WORD Callers

WORD Callers

Small-Group and One-to-One
Interventions for Children Who
"Read" but Don't Comprehend

KELLY B. CARTWRIGHT

HEINEMANN   Portsmouth, NH

Heinemann
361 Hanover Street
Portsmouth, NH 03801–3912
www.heinemann.com

Offices and agents throughout the world

The author and publisher wish to thank those who have generously given permission to reprint borrowed material:

Figure 6–1 adapted from "Group Story Mapping: A Comprehension Strategy for Both Skilled and Unskilled Readers" by Lorna Idol from *Journal of Learning Disabilities*, Vol. 20, No. 4, April 1987. Published by Sage Publications. Reprinted by permission of the publishers.

Figure 8–2 adapted from "A Teacher Development Project in Transitional Strategy Instruction for Teachers of Severely Reading-Disabled Adolescents" by Valerie Anderson from *Teaching and Teacher Education*, Vol. 8, No. 4, August 1992. Published by Elsevier. Reprinted by permission of the publisher.

Figure 8–3 adapted from "The Road Not Yet Taken: A Transactional Strategies Approach to Comprehension Instruction" by Rachel Brown from *The Reading Teacher*, Vol. 61, No. 7, April 2008. Published by the International Reading Association. Reprinted by permission of the publisher.

Library of Congress Cataloging-in-Publication Data
Cartwright, Kelly B.
  Word callers : small-group and one-to-one interventions for children who read but don't comprehend / Kelly B. Cartwright.
       p. cm. – (Research-informed classroom series)
  Includes bibliographical references.
  ISBN-13: 978-0-325-02693-0
  ISBN-10: 0-325-02693-9
  1. Reading—Remedial teaching. 2. Reading comprehension.
3. Individualized instruction.   I. Title.

LB1050.5.C34 2010
372.43—dc22   2010018760

———————————————————————————

Editor: Wendy Murray
Production: Vicki Kasabian
Interior design: Catherine Arakelian
Interior photographs and author photograph: Adam Baker
Cover photograph: Zigy Kaluzny/Stone Collection/Getty Images
Cover design: Lisa A. Fowler
Illustrator: Rita Lascaro
Typesetter: Kim Arney
Manufacturing: Valerie Cooper

Printed in the United States of America on acid-free paper

14 13 12 11 10 ML 1 2 3 4 5

For my daughter, Jessie,
who was my first and best
teacher of how children
think, learn, and learn to read.

CONTENTS

CONTENTS

PREFACE

All struggling readers are not the same. In this book I share current research and instructional practices for those children we've come to call *word callers*. These are the children who can read like a dream, with impressive fluency, but would be hard pressed to tell you what the text was about. Their high decoding skills and comparatively low comprehension have puzzled researchers and educators for decades. These bright, capable struggling learners crop up in just about every classroom and have been noticed around the globe and across grade levels. Some studies have estimated that word callers make up as much as one third of all struggling readers. Yet discovering just what is awry in their cognitive processes—and what teachers can do to set these children on the right path—is far from common knowledge. That is, until now!

In this book I share recent research and interventions that have helped these children to make the shift from decoding alone to reading with understanding. My own research and interventions are relatively new, as are some of the other interventions I share in this book; others you will find in these pages have been around a while longer, but they aren't yet part of many teachers' and reading specialists' repertoires. My hope in writing this text is to share insights into what makes word callers tick, as well as interventions that are effective in improving these children's comprehension, so that we can help them learn to enjoy the rich meaningful world of reading that they are missing.

It's not often in education that we have such a storybook scenario to helping our at-risk learners, but as you read this book, you too will be excited by the evidence; and when you try the classroom strategies and interventions with children, the outcome will be decidedly positive. Once these children go from "just reading words" to being able to crack open the meaning of a text, the world is their oyster. Reading becomes a pleasurable experience they seek out, and with a teacher guiding them to books at their appropriate levels, they "turn around" and begin to rack up the benefits of reading, from building vocabulary and conceptual knowledge to engagement with the memorable characters of children's literature.

The Time Is Now

When I set out to write this book, RTI (Response to Intervention) was a mere seedling. Now it's in full flower and schools are trying to find the most thoughtful, well-researched interventions available, so that students who struggle can get the early, intensive boost they need to get on grade level and flourish. The timing of this book couldn't be better, for the interventions in this book are research-tested and developed by educators who were studying struggling readers long before the RTI mandate. Similarly, with its tiered approach to instruction, RTI has raised our awareness of differentiated instruction, and along with that, the instructional potency of small-group instruction. The interventions and lessons in this book were indeed designed for needs-based, small-group teaching and learning as well as one-to-one settings.

A Variety of Interventions to Try

Just as not all struggling readers are the same, the practices or interventions we use to help them are not the same. Word callers are a particular type of struggling reader, and even within this group, each child is unique, and what helps each child make the shift to meaning is unique. However, as I describe in Chapter 1, what many word callers have in common is an "inflexible" approach to print. They're so focused on the letters and decoding, their minds don't bend and stretch enough to knit together the meaning of the words they are reading. The diverse interventions in this book all address this inflexibility, helping these children become more cognitively flexible and better able to process meaning alongside letter-sound information. You'll gain a "variety pack" of classroom practices, from ones as simple as using riddles and other ambiguous language to those as complex as Transactional Strategies Instruction (TSI), wherein you integrate metacognitive strategies during your lessons, something that may take you a little more time to get down pat.

My Assessment and Intervention: The Power of Word and Picture Cards

A centerpiece of this book is the Sound-Meaning Flexible Thinking Assessment and Intervention, a method that involves the accompanying word and picture cards, and one you can use to remarkable effect with your word callers. You can use these cards individually with children (especially useful for reading specialists), or if you're a classroom teacher you can use them with small groups. My research has shown that in as few as five lessons, word callers begin to "unglue from print" and become much more able to attend to meaning.

It's fortuitous timing to bring this assessment and intervention to classroom teachers and reading specialists when RTI is on everyone's mind. It can be tough to know which resources are really effective—and for which children they are best suited. With the sound-meaning assessment and lessons, you can be assured of a firm research base to help your "word caller" children.

A Simple Assessment

The assessment tells you which children have difficulty focusing on words' sounds and meanings at once, which impairs children's ability to get meaning from text. And, your classroom assessments may also indicate the children who are high on decoding fluency but relatively low on comprehension.

The Lessons

The sound-meaning sorting lessons help change the way these children think about print by *requiring* that they coordinate words' meanings and sounds. That is, the lessons help word callers wrap their minds around both decoding and meaning, enabling them to make the critical shift to meaning-focused reading. Effective in multiple formats, the sound-meaning lessons can be delivered in a typical small-group format in weekly 20- to 30-minute sessions for up to five children at a time. However, for word callers who may need extra help, these lessons can be used more intensively with individual children in 10- to 15-minute daily lessons.

Taken together, the collection of research-tested interventions in this book provides a wide variety of ways to reach a group of struggling readers for whom we have typically had few instructional resources. Despite their variety, the common goal of these interventions is to *open children's minds to meaning* by helping them think more flexibly about print, giving them access to the rich world of reading that has been just out of their reach.

ACKNOWLEDGMENTS

As you might expect, a project like this takes a great deal of time and the support of many people. I have had much help and encouragement along the way, without which this book would not have been possible. First, I must thank Nell Duke for encouraging me to think broadly about how word callers can be supported with research-based practices and for inviting me to be part of the Research-Informed Classroom series. Nell introduced me to Wendy Murray, my amazing editor at Heinemann, whose creativity and insights have stretched my thinking about the ideas in this book and about what it means to write about research for the teachers who use it. Thank you, Wendy, for challenging me in constructive ways and for your positive guidance of this project from its inception. Thanks, too, to all of the other terrific people in Heinemann's production, design, editing, and marketing departments—Vicki Kasabian, Stephanie Turner, Catherine Arakelian, Eric Chalek, and others—who helped make this book a reality. Your support and enthusiasm for *Word Callers* is much appreciated!

My circle of support is broader than my editors. I can't thank my family, friends, and colleagues enough for sharing me with this book for the many months (okay, years) that it has consumed my time. I owe a debt of gratitude to my mother, Sue Branam, who taught me at an early age to love words and to love books, and who read *every word* of my first draft of this book. Thanks for your eagle eyes, Mom! Likewise, I must thank my father, Walter "Rookie" Branam, whose perpetual encouragement and advice have been (and continue to be) invaluable in this project and in life. Additionally, I must thank other supporters and colleagues who have listened, challenged, tried my work in their classrooms, allowed me to learn from their students, and inspired my thinking, including my sister and greatest cheerleader, Jenny King; research collaborator, Tim Marshall; wise friend, Sandy Lopater, who encouraged me to "write a little bit every day"; and reading colleagues Donna Savage, Ken Schmidt, Jan Clause, Kathy Bohince, Sherry Edbauer, Shirley Bever, Joan Payne, and Cathy Huemer. I also owe a special thank-you to Adam Baker and the students and teachers who shared their time for our picture day photo shoot.

Finally, I am most grateful to the classroom teachers, reading specialists, interventionists, literacy coaches, and school administrators who will read this book and try the interventions in its pages. I am ever amazed by your unwavering, daily commitment to promoting students' literacy learning. Your passion for growing readers and for finding new ways to reach our struggling students is truly inspiring. Thank you for helping children to see that reading is *more* than just the words.

Word Callers
What to Watch For

1

Word callers. We all have them in our classrooms. These students often surprise us (and their parents) because when we ask them to read, they read aloud expressively and typically have little difficulty with decoding, leading us to believe they have reading down pat. My preservice teachers are always quite puzzled when I assign these students to them for tutoring because it seems, at first blush, that they can read very well. However, when we ask these children to tell us about a story they have just read, they simply are not able to do so! I recently gave a talk on word callers at our state reading conference, and a reading specialist approached me after the talk to share the following story of one of her students, whom we will call Matthew (a pseudonym).

> I was sent a fifth grader named Matthew who was having comprehension problems. Matthew was a wonderful "reader." In fact, he "read" beautifully—he word called fluently! One day, after providing a remarkably expressive oral reading of a paragraph, I asked him, "Can you tell me what the paragraph meant?" The student replied, in an exasperated tone, "You mean I have to understand what it means, too?" (Lynch 2009)

For Matthew, and for many students like him, reading is a "case of words *or* meaning" (Dolch 1960, 189). Students like Matthew have traditionally been labeled "word callers" because they call out words from a page, often rendering fluent oral readings of texts, with little to no comprehension—what Dolch (1960) called "meaningless reading" (150). According to

We keep meaning foremost. But the children still must know the words. It is not a case of words or meaning. It is a case of meaning and words.

EDWARD DOLCH,
TEACHING PRIMARY READING

Chall (1996), as children develop as readers during the primary grades, they typically focus on print in order to become fluent decoders. Then, as decoding begins to require fewer mental resources, children's focus shifts from learning *how* to read (or decode) to reading to learn new things (i.e., reading for understanding). Although many researchers believe that students should be encouraged to focus on meaning from the beginning (e.g., Biemiller 2001, 2003; Hart and Risley 1995), Chall (1996, 46) suggested that children typically "unglue" from print sometime around third to fourth grade so that they can focus more fully on meaning. Some children may make that shift earlier or later, depending on their level of decoding fluency. As you have probably surmised, word callers have trouble making that shift, which some have suggested contributes to the decline of reading performance in fourth grade, typically called the fourth-grade slump (Chall 1996; Hirsch 2003; Leach, Scarborough, and Rescorla 2003). Some researchers who study these children call them "poor comprehenders" because they show surprisingly poor comprehension in comparison to their age-appropriate decoding skills (e.g., see Cain and Oakhill 2003; Nation 2005; Oakhill 1993; and Oakhill and Yuill 1996 for reviews). Often, despite our best efforts, these children still display a surprising lack of attention to meaning, which leaves us with some important questions, such as:

- How many of our struggling readers fall into this category of word callers?
- What are the characteristics of word callers?
- Is there something about these students' prior instruction that leads them to focus on words instead of meaning?
- Why don't these students grasp the meanings of the texts they read?
- And, most important, how can we help these students understand that reading is about meaning?

Children who fall into this particular segment of the "struggling reader" category are strikingly consistent in their belief that reading is about decoding, and teachers and researchers across the globe recognize these children's misguided focus on words. Word callers have been identified and studied in the U.K. (Cain and Oakhill 2007; Yuill and Oakhill 1991), France (Megherbi and Ehrlich 2005), Italy (Levorato, Roch, and Nesi 2007), Canada (Lesaux, Lipka, and Siegel 2006), and the United States (Riddle Buly and Valencia 2002). Yet, little research has been done on how to effectively set these children on the right path. I recently heard from a reading teacher in Nebraska who reported that the fourth- to sixth-grade students at one of the schools in her district had wonderful decoding skills (scoring over 90 percent on decoding accuracy) and relatively poor comprehension (a sobering 50 percent; Chalupa 2008). When I share these percentages at conferences and in schools, I see nods of recognition from teachers, reading specialists, literacy coaches, teachers' aides, and building administrators—virtually everyone involved in the process of developing literacy skills for students.

Whether you teach first grade or fifth, children who are reading fluently with little or no understanding are probably not developing reading comprehension skills because they are inflexible in the way they approach print. That is, they are likely to be focusing passively on one aspect—usually words' sounds—to the exclusion of other important aspects like meaning (Cartwright 2002; Dewitz and Dewitz 2003; Yuill and Oakhill 1991). Even typical readers have a tendency to focus inflexibly on the letters in words and not their meanings. When typical second- to fifth-grade readers were asked what they would tell a friend who had trouble with reading, the most common responses by far (48 percent of the 673 responses) focused on word-level features (Mesmer, Dredger, and Barksdale 2008). Children said that they would tell the friend to "sound it out" or "pronounce it," or to look at the spelling, letters, or words. Of those 673 responses, only fifteen (2 percent) suggested that the friend pay attention to meaning!

In fact, work in child development shows that elementary-aged children have a tendency to focus on the sounds of printed words and have difficulty switching their attention to meaning (Bialystok and Niccols 1989). This tendency is problematic for young readers because good comprehension requires that they take a step back and also consider meaning. Most children have no trouble making this shift. However, some children seem to be super-glued to print. For these children reading is equivalent to decoding, and they demonstrate a significant lack of attention to meaning. Skilled readers, on the other hand, are able to pay attention to, and coordinate flexibly, many features of print at once, such as meaning, syntax, strategic and metacognitive processes, and, of course, words' letters and their associated sounds (Adams 1990; National Reading Panel 2000; Pressley 2006a). We have known of the existence of word callers for over four decades (Dolch 1960). And, although teachers around the globe recognize these children in their classrooms, these children "have not been widely studied" (Aaron, Joshi, and Williams 1999, 130), and there are few published resources that focus on interventions designed to help these children achieve a more flexible approach to print.

Overview of This Book

The good news is, we can help these children. I am compelled to write this book on the heels of promising research on what is awry with these students' processes. I also want to share research-tested ideas for helping word callers make the shift from decoding-focused to meaning-focused reading. In this book, I share recent research on children's and adults' thinking that provides insights into the nature of—and interventions for—word callers' difficulties. This research has important implications for helping word callers make the critical shift they need to become good comprehenders.

In this chapter, I will review research that indicates how many of our struggling readers are word callers. Then, I will describe features of word callers derived from decades of research in the U.K. and the U.S. (see, e.g., Cain and Oakhill 2003; Nation 2005; Oakhill 1993; and Oakhill and Yuill 1996 for reviews). To close the chapter, I will discuss instructional practices that may lead children to focus too heavily on print and not enough on meaning.

In Chapter 2, I will describe new work on children's thinking that provides insight into word callers' difficulties.

In the remaining chapters of the book, I will share strategies that help word callers understand that reading is about meaning. In Chapter 3 I will present a research-tested technique that allows you to assess your word callers' levels of flexible thinking and compare them to expected levels. The bulk of the text, Chapters 4 to 7, will focus on research-tested interventions that are particularly effective in addressing word callers' difficulties by increasing attention to other features of print besides letter-sound information (see Gersten et al. 2001 and Wanzek and Vaughn 2007 for reviews of effective, research-tested interventions for struggling readers). Finally, in Chapter 8, I share an instructional approach that helps word callers (and other students) understand the active, strategic meaning-focused nature of skilled comprehenders' processing. These interventions provide extra support for word callers in thinking about sounds and meanings of print, creating mental images of text, understanding and using story structure, making inferences about texts' meanings, and actively engaging in strategic comprehension processes. In each of these chapters I will suggest ways to incorporate these techniques into your daily classroom routines.

How Many Word Callers?

For many years, we have placed all of our struggling readers together in the "low group" for reading instruction. This kind of general ability or level-based grouping reflects a tendency to think about these children as having the same sorts of difficulties. All struggling readers, however, are not the same (Flood et al. 1992). These children have different profiles of literacy subskills, some with weak decoding skills, others with low levels of fluency, and still others with poor comprehension despite adequate decoding and fluency. Even within these categories there may be important differences, such as poor comprehension due to weak vocabulary and background knowledge versus poor comprehension due to lack of strategy use. And, because struggling readers have different, specific difficulties, they benefit from different, specific types of instruction (McCoach, O'Connell, and Levitt 2006; Tomlinson 1999). If you have ever worked with word callers in your classroom, you know that they typically do not respond to instruction in the same way as their peers—even other struggling readers with different kinds of reading difficulties.

Patterns of Reading Skill in Your Classroom: Research Highlights to Help You

Because all struggling readers are not the same, several researchers have attempted to identify the various patterns of difficulty that exist, so that we might better address these children's particular strengths and needs in our educational practice. In each of these studies, groups of children with high decoding skills and comparatively low comprehension—that is, word callers—emerged. In this section I briefly describe the gist of several of these studies and indicate the percentages of struggling readers in each study that fit the word caller profile. In addition, to help you place word callers in the broader context of reading variation in your classroom, Figure 1–1 provides a chart that describes the profiles of readers discovered in the research described below, which divides students according to levels of decoding skill, reading rate, and comprehension. In this book our focus is on the children identified as word callers—the groups at the top of the second column in Figure 1–1 who are relatively high on decoding and fluency but low on comprehension. Please note that although this chart is a useful rubric for thinking about patterns of reading skill in your classroom, each of your students may not fit neatly into these categories. Individual assessment is always the best guide for instructional decision making.

- Applegate, Applegate, and Modla (2009) studied 171 teacher-identified highly fluent readers in grades 2 through 10 to examine the relation between fluency and comprehension. These researchers were inspired by a classroom teacher who identified one of her students as her "best reader, for sure. She's just not a good comprehender" (Applegate, Applegate, and Modla 2009, 512). This word caller was judged to be the best reader in the class! Applegate and colleagues found that *a full third of the highly fluent readers in their study were struggling comprehenders—that is, they were word callers*—reminding us that decoding, fluency, and comprehension do not necessarily go hand in hand. This story also is a wake-up call that teachers themselves sometimes equate fluent and fast with best, an unfortunate reality.

FIGURE 1–1

Profiles of Struggling Readers

		Good Comprehension	Poor Comprehension
Strong Word Identification and Decoding (accurate)	**High Reading Rate** (faster readers)	Strong Readers	Automatic Word Callers
	Low Reading Rate (slower readers)	Average Readers	Slow Word Callers
Moderate Word Identification and Decoding (less accurate)	**High Reading Rate** (faster readers)		Struggling Word Callers
	Low Reading Rate (slower readers)	Slow and Steady Comprehenders	Poor Readers
Poor Word Identification and Decoding (inaccurate)	**Low Reading Rate** (slower readers)	Word Stumblers	Disabled Readers

This chart provides a glimpse of the tremendous variety in the sources of readers' difficulties and strengths. These groupings are based on research on profiles of struggling readers reviewed in Chapter 1; labels for groups of students were derived from studies by Riddle Buly and Valencia (2002) and Torppa et al. (2007). Reading rate was typically assessed in these studies as words read per minute; it thus focused on fast, automatic reading. Accuracy of reading was assessed with measures of nonword decoding and word identification. Finally, measures of vocabulary skill were used with measures of comprehension to indicate meaning-focused readers in Riddle Buly and Valencia's (2002) work. Please note that individual students may not fit neatly into these categories; individual assessment is always the best guide for instruction.

- Torppa et al. (2007) studied 1750 Finnish children across first and second grades. They found five different profiles of readers: good readers (176 children), average readers (692 children), slow decoders (411 children), poor comprehenders (179 children), and poor readers (210 children who struggled with both decoding and comprehension). *Word callers (what the researchers called poor comprehenders) made up 22 percent of the children with reading difficulty in this study.*

- Catts, Hogan, and Fey (2003) studied second-grade struggling readers in the midwestern United States who had particular difficulty with comprehension. The students were part of a larger study because they had exhibited language impairments in kindergarten. The researchers found that 28.8 percent of poor comprehenders still had good decoding skills—that is, *almost a third of their poor comprehenders were classified as word callers!*

- Riddle Buly and Valencia (2002) studied struggling readers who had failed state assessments and found six different types of struggling readers, including three types of word callers. Each of the groups of word callers demonstrated high decoding skill relative to their vocabulary and comprehension.

  - Eighteen percent of the struggling readers in their study were "automatic word callers"—children who were fluent readers and who had no difficulty with decoding but who had surprisingly weak comprehension.

  - An additional 15 percent of children were characterized as "struggling word callers." These children were not quite as skilled at decoding, but they self-corrected reliably, resulting in fairly accurate decoding and good fluency, with surprisingly poor comprehension.

  - Finally, 17 percent of the struggling readers were characterized as "slow word callers"—children who had high decoding skill despite their poor comprehension, and who were also lower in fluency than the other word callers in the study. These children may struggle with comprehension because they have not yet developed automaticity in decoding, leaving few mental resources to focus on comprehension (LaBerge and Samuels 1974), but these children may also lack the requisite strategic processes necessary to make the shift to meaning-focused reading, similar to their faster-reading word caller peers.

  Taken together, these findings show that *word callers made up at least one third of the struggling readers in this study.*

- Aaron, Joshi, and Williams (1999) examined the profiles of three small groups of struggling readers. The first group of 16 struggling readers was drawn from a larger group of volunteers in third, fourth, and sixth grades from midsized towns in the southeastern United States. Two of these were word callers (12.5 percent). The second group of struggling readers was chosen from a Title I classroom, and seven of twelve of these students (58 percent) were word callers. The third group of struggling readers included eleven students who attended a University Reading Clinic. Of these, two were word callers (18 percent). *Across the three groups in this study, almost a third of the struggling readers (28 percent) were word callers.*

- In 1999 Shankweiler and colleagues also examined profiles of struggling readers who were recruited from a variety of locations in the United States as part of a larger study on learning problems (Shankweiler et al. 1999). Parents responded to the call for participants, and 361 children were included in the study. The profiles of these readers were similar to those discovered by Torppa et al. (2007) in their study of Finnish children. There were thirty-two poor decoders, seventeen poor comprehenders, 127 poor readers, and 114 good readers. The remaining seventy-one children seemed to fit the description of Torppa and colleagues' "average readers." In this study, *9.6 percent of the struggling readers were word callers.*

When considered together, studies investigating profiles of reading difficulties show that roughly one tenth to one third of our struggling readers are word callers. That is no small number. Based on the studies we reviewed here, I suspect that the proportion of word callers in the general population of struggling readers is closer to a third than to a tenth. The majority of these studies indicated that about a third of struggling readers are word callers, and Shankweiler and colleagues' study (which found that 10 percent of struggling readers were word callers) included a restricted group of children who were nominated by parents because they had learning problems. Thus, the children in that study were probably not representative of the broad group of struggling readers in typical classrooms.

Defining Characteristics

Physically, word callers look like any other children in our classrooms. Behaviorally these children look like good readers because they can decode fluently, which makes identifying them a little tricky. Generally, word callers are children who demonstrate age-appropriate decoding skill with comparatively low comprehension. More specifically, word callers differ from their peers with better comprehension in particular ways. Researchers in the United Kingdom (and a few of their colleagues in other countries, including the United States) have been studying these children for decades, finding a number of skills with which word callers seem to have difficulty. I will briefly describe these differences here in order to provide a picture of word callers' problems so that we have a basis for discussing potential solutions later in the book. Before we get started, it is important to note that word callers do *not* differ from their peers with better comprehension on general cognitive ability (Nation and Snowling 2000; Nation, Clarke, and Snowling 2002), word reading speed (Nation and Snowling 1998; Yuill and Oakhill 1991), word reading accuracy and automaticity (Yuill and Oakhill 1991), short-term memory (Oakhill, Yuill, and Parkin 1986), and memory for exact wording of sentences (Oakhill 1982). And, their comprehension difficulties do not relate to differences in general knowledge (Cain et al. 2001). In short, word callers are bright children who are similar to their peers in many ways but have difficulty with particular aspects of literacy tasks. The following list describes the kinds of difficulties faced by these children.

- Word callers tend to have lower vocabulary knowledge—that is, knowledge of words' meanings—than their peers who are better comprehenders (Ricketts, Nation, and Bishop 2007).

- Word callers are less sensitive to meaningful relations among words (Nation and Snowling 1999), which means that they have more trouble categorizing words according to meaning.

- Word callers have difficulty inferring the meanings of unknown words from context (Oakhill 1983). For example, when reading a text about the life cycle of a butterfly, word callers would have a more difficult time figuring out the meaning for monarch (a type of butterfly) in the following sentence: *The monarch came out of the chrysalis and spread its new wings.*

- Word callers have more difficulty constructing meaning from orally presented sentences than their peers with better comprehension (Oakhill 1982). They hear the sounds, but they don't always process the meaning.

- When asked to arrange words into sentences that make sense, word callers have more difficulty than their peers because word callers are less aware of appropriate syntax—the proper arrangement of words necessary to create meaning (Nation and Snowling 2000).

- Word callers are less likely to monitor their own understanding while reading than students with better comprehension, suggesting that word callers are lower in metacognition than their more skilled counterparts (Ehrlich, Remond, and Tardieu 1999; Oakhill, Hartt, and Samols 2005; Paris and Myers 1981).

- Even when word callers have world knowledge related to a text's content, they have difficulty making connections between their own prior knowledge and text (Dewitz and Dewitz 2003). For example, read the following sentence: *When she looked in her basket, Sally was upset to find that she had forgotten the salt.* What kind of basket did Sally have? In answering this question you probably used your prior knowledge of baskets, especially those that might contain food, and probably guessed that Sally had a picnic basket. (Some of my students have suggested that *shopping basket* would also be a good answer to this question.) But, word callers are much less likely to access their background knowledge to make sense of texts.

- Good readers must use information in text to make inferences about text content that is not actually written. In a narrative about a boy who was late to school, Yuill and Oakhill (1991, 71) stated that "He started pedaling to school as fast as he could." You probably inferred that the boy was riding a bicycle, as would any good reader. Word callers, however, have difficulty making these kinds of inferences when reading (Cain and Oakhill 1999; Cain et al. 2001; Cain, Oakhill, and Lemmon 2004; Oakhill and Yuill 1986; Oakhill, Yuill, and Parkin 1986; Yuill and Oakhill 1991).

- Readers sometimes encounter ambiguous language or inconsistencies in text, and word callers have difficulty resolving these situations successfully in order to preserve meaning (August, Flavell, and Clift 1984; Garner and Kraus 1981; Megherbi and Ehrlich 2005; Oakhill, Hartt, and Samols 2005; Yuill and Oakhill 1988; Yuill, Oakhill, and Parkin 1989; Zabrucky 1990; Zabrucky and Moore 1989).

- Finally, although word callers do not differ from better comprehenders on some tests of working memory, the part of our memory that allows us to hold information in mind while working on part of that information (Oakhill, Yuill, and Parkin 1986; Stothard and Hulme 1992; see Bayliss et al. 2005 for a description of working memory), word callers have trouble with other, related thinking tasks that require them to deliberately control attention in particular ways (Swanson, Howard, and Sáez 2007). For example, when reading passages that contain inconsistent bits of information, word callers can deliberately detect the inconsistencies when the inconsistent pieces of information are close together in the text. But, if the inconsistent bits of information are separated by greater distance (i.e., by more words or sentences), these children have more trouble finding them than their peers with better comprehension (Oakhill, Hartt, and Samols 2005; Yuill, Oakhill, and Parkin 1989). (See Chapter 2 for more on working memory and its relation to reading comprehension.)

Why the Focus on Words Instead of Meaning?

Some prominent researchers have suggested that an instructional focus on fluent decoding produces speedy, accurate readers who do not understand what they read, which sounds a lot like our description of word callers (Allington 2006; Pressley, Hilden, and Shankland 2005). And, even when children achieve high fluency scores on the DIBELS (Dynamic Indicators of Basic Literacy Skills) fluency assessment, reading many words per minute, these students do not show comparably good comprehension (Pressley, Hilden, and Shankland 2005). So, speedy reading does not ensure reading for meaning.

Further, we know that teachers tend to focus more on word-level decoding processes than on more complex, meaning-focused instruction when they work with struggling readers (Allington 1980; Chinn et al. 1993; also see Mertzman 2008), which might lead struggling readers to adopt word-focused, rather than meaning-focused, reading strategies. Moreover, when students demonstrate fluent decoding, they are less likely to be identified as struggling readers, even when they struggle with comprehension. Take, for example, the teacher who commented that one fluent decoder was her "best reader" despite inadequate comprehension (Applegate, Applegate, and Modla 2009, 512). Thus, word callers may not get the meaning-focused instructional support they need.

Certainly, we cannot conclude that all word callers struggle with comprehension because of the kinds of instruction they may have received. Some children simply have more difficulty processing meaning than their peers. Instruction is important, though, and quality instruction is not one-size-fits-all. As we have learned in this chapter, all struggling readers are not the same. And, students make more reading gains when instruction is matched precisely to individual students' particular needs (Connor et al. 2007; Connor, Morrison, and Slominski 2006; Connor et al. 2009; Juel and Minden-Cupp 2000); therefore, a decoding-focused approach does not work for all struggling learners, especially those who have good decoding skills and struggle with comprehension. The good news is that when struggling comprehenders do receive quality meaning-focused instruction, such as the techniques presented in this book, their comprehension improves (e.g., Anderson 1992; Brown et al. 1996; Cartwright, Clause, and Schmidt 2007; Levin 1973; McGee and Johnson 2003; Oakhill and Patel 1991; Yuill 1996, 2007).

Closing Notes

As you can see, word callers have particular difficulty with meaning, whether it is meaningful relations between words, meanings of sentences, or monitoring their own understanding of a text's meaning. However, word callers are bright children whose general cognitive ability, text memory, and word reading speed are generally unimpaired, as is their ability to fluently decode text. They have many strengths on which to draw. Yet, word callers seem to have "tunnel vision." They passively and inflexibly focus on word-level features of text and somehow miss texts' meanings. In the remainder of this book we will examine new research on children's thinking that will inform our understanding of word callers' difficulties, and we will explore ways to assess and improve these children's active and flexible thinking, enabling them to break away from print and focus on meaning for improved comprehension.

How Does This Help You?

Questions to Consider

- Do you have students now who seem to fit the word caller profile? List some attributes that make you think so.

- Is there a practice you've tried that seemed to help the students "catch up" their comprehension to their fluency? Why do you think the practice was effective?

The High-Low Paradox

New Cognitive Science Research on Why These Children Struggle

When I began graduate school, my daughter, Jessie, was just over a year old. It was amazing to be studying literacy and language acquisition in tandem with experiencing Jessie move from babbling to single words—and then daily, it seemed she could add more and more words to her vocabulary. But what amazed me even more is what she could do with those words, and the concepts they represented. One day she was toddling through the kitchen and spied a bright green apple on the kitchen table. Now, she had never seen a green apple before—she had only seen red ones. So, you can imagine my surprise when she peeked up at the table and said "apple," as plain as day. (She actually pronounced the word *abble*.) I wondered: How did she know this? She had never seen a green apple before! She had somehow developed a concept of appleness that was flexible enough to apply beyond the red apples she ate on a regular basis. I realized then that children's thinking was more complex than I had assumed. As teachers, we see evidence of children's thinking surpassing our expectations—or surprising us when it diverges from what we expect—and yet we don't always know what to do with it to advance their learning. Who hasn't been bowled over by the inferential thinking of a preschooler or elementary-aged child—some moment when a connection they make seems years ahead of the class, the curriculum, our expectations. The best teachers teach in ways that invite and advance students to learn at this outmost edge, so to speak.

But let's return to children that fall into the word caller category, those who can seem almost ahead of the curve in fluency but far behind on comprehension. What's going on in their brains? Fortunately for us, new insights about children's thought processes can tell us much.

In recent decades, research on children's thinking has exploded. Fields in the Learning Sciences, such as cognitive development, neuroscience, and educational psychology, have revealed much about how the mind works and about how children's thinking and learning processes develop (Sawyer 2006). New research on children's thinking has sought answers to questions such as the following:

- Why do some children understand others' perspectives, while other children do not?

- How do children acquire and store new knowledge?

- What kinds of mental habits are necessary for children to complete academic tasks successfully?

- How do children learn to process complicated tasks that involve multiple features, such as reading or math?

Cognitive Flexibility: All Good Readers Have It, Why Word Callers Don't

Answers to each of these questions provide useful insights into the thinking processes of our word-calling students. Because reading is a thinking—or cognitive—task, it makes sense that new discoveries about children's thinking would have important implications for understanding how children think about reading. But, little research has been done to investigate these implications (Siegler 2000; Sternberg and Lyon 2002). As I noted in Chapter 1, the purpose of this book is to build a bridge across these areas to shed some light on the particular reading problems of word callers. In this chapter I will describe briefly some of the answers to the questions listed above, with particular attention to how these answers apply to word callers' thinking processes. As I do so, I will draw on examples of real children and classrooms to yield five critical insights about word callers' thinking.

Why Do Some Children Understand Others' Perspectives, While Other Children Don't?

If you have ever interacted with preschoolers, you know that they sometimes do very odd things because they can't seem to grasp what others know. One day, when Jessie was almost three years old, she was looking at a picture book, seated in a chair across the room from me. As she looked intently at the page she was "reading," she pointed to the book and asked, "Mommy, what's that?" Of course,

I couldn't see what she was viewing in the book—all I saw was the cover. She had no awareness that my visual perspective might be different from hers. Now, consider my little friend "Sam" (a pseudonym). When he was about four years old, he was an avid hide-and-seek player. He would have me count for him, and he would run and hide. When it was time for me to look for him, invariably, I would round a corner in search of Sam and find him in exactly the same spot in which he had hidden just moments before.

In both of these examples we see children who do not yet understand other people's viewpoints. Jessie did not understand that my visual perspective, and the knowledge I could get from what I could see, was different from her own. Sam did not understand that I already had knowledge that would affect the game: I already knew about his favorite spot, so he should have chosen a different spot for hiding. In both of these examples, the children were unable to hold two perspectives in mind at once: their own view of the world and my view of the world. Piaget called young preschoolers like Jessie and Sam egocentric, not because they were selfish, but because he observed that they were quite literally unable to take others' perspectives (Piaget and Inhelder 1966/1969).

Researchers interested in this unusual behavior (unusual by adult standards, anyway—it's typical for preschoolers) have discovered that in the preschool years children begin to develop a theory of mind—an understanding of how their own and others' minds work (Astington, Harris, and Olson 1988; Flavell 2004; Wellman and Liu 2004). As part of the development of a theory of mind, children become aware of their own thoughts and that their thoughts can differ from the world. (For example, I understand that I can think my keys are in my purse when they might really be on the kitchen counter.) The ability to think about one's own thoughts enables important skills like metacognition and strategic behavior, which are important for reading comprehension. We will turn to these a bit later in the book.

In the process of developing an understanding of their own and others' minds, children also learn that their beliefs, knowledge, and thoughts can be different from what others believe, know, or think. This understanding enables them to do things like deceive their siblings or surprise their parents. I still remember the moment at which I realized that Jessie was developing a theory of mind: it was my birthday, and she and her father had just returned from purchasing a cake. My birthday is in October, and the cake had a jack-o'-lantern face on top. Five-year-old Jessie could barely contain her excitement. "Mommy," she said, "we bought you a cake, and it has (imagine a weighty pause as Jessie caught herself before spilling the beans) yellow flowers all over it!" Jessie was, at that moment, able to keep two thoughts in mind at once—the information about what was really on the cake, and the fact that I did not yet know this information—and she was able to use what she knew about the two thoughts to conceal a surprise.

As this example illustrates, developing a theory of mind requires that children consider at least two perspectives at once. This is an important accomplishment because it marks the point in development when children are capable of multiple representation—the ability to hold two ideas (or mental representations) in mind at the same time. When I teach this concept to preservice teachers, I show them Figure 2–1, which provides a visual representation of a younger, less flexible child who can focus on only one idea at a time and an older, more flexible child who is able to hold more than one idea in mind at a time. (My students and I typically call these the "lightbulb head children" because they have bright ideas, and because of their uniquely shaped heads!)

FIGURE 2–1

Flexible and Inflexible Thinkers

Although the social world provides children much of their initial practice with multiple representational ability (Astington, Harris, and Olson 1988; Gopnik, Meltzoff, and Kuhl 1999), this skill contributes to many other areas of development, such as language learning (Flavell 1988) and academic skills (Arlin 1981). And, although the acquisition of a theory of mind marks the beginning of this development in preschool, elementary school children—and even adults—vary in the ability to hold multiple ideas in mind at once (Cartwright 2007; Cartwright, Isaac, and Dandy 2006; Kuhn and Pease 2006). In addition, when the ideas to be considered are quite different from one another, or if they seem to conflict with one another, holding them both in mind is more difficult (Jacques and Zelazo 2005; Kloo and Perner 2003). This point is especially important when we consider the wide variety of ideas children must keep in mind to be successful readers.

Now consider Andrew, who is in third grade and is reading a book with a few classmates in a small-group reading lesson. His teacher, Mrs. Riley, has asked him and his peers to use the imagery strategy while reading, and she instructs them to make a mental picture of the events in the story. (Andrew and his teacher are not real individuals. Rather, he and Mrs. Riley represent many children and teachers I have observed.) Andrew is a fairly fluent reader, and he decodes well. He hears Mrs. Riley's directions, but as he reads his thinking is focused on the process of decoding the words on the page. Like Jessie and Sam (and the right-hand child in Figure 2–1), Andrew's focus is on only one aspect of the situation at hand. In order to engage in the imagery strategy, Andrew and his peers must think about their own reading processes and focus on (at least) two aspects of the reading task: decoding the words and picturing the meaning. Comprehension strategies like imagery require that children engage in metacognition, or thinking about their own thinking (Block and Pressley 2001; Israel et al. 2005), which requires them to consider multiple ideas about the reading task. Word callers like Andrew are reliably able to keep one aspect of reading in mind, the letter-sound information used while decoding, and they read fluently as a result. Adding a second mental representation to the mix, however, such as one about meaning, is quite difficult for these children, especially because meaning is very different from letter-sound information.

> **INSIGHT 1:** Word callers have difficulty considering more than one idea at a time. They focus on letter-sound information, and have difficulty also considering meaning.

How Do Children Acquire and Store New Knowledge?

As we observed in Chapter 1, children sometimes have ideas about reading that do not match our adult conceptions. Struggling readers sometimes think that reading is about pronouncing words correctly and avoiding mistakes (Gaskins and Gaskins 1997; Yuill and Oakhill 1991), and even typical readers are more likely to suggest that successful reading is about letters, sounds, and spelling than about meaning (Mesmer et al. 2008). Children who grow up in a literate culture begin to build knowledge about reading even before they enter school (Teale and Sulzby 1986; Whitehurst and Lonigan 1998), and children's knowledge and beliefs about reading affect the way they approach learning to read (Durik, Vida, and Eccles 2006; Paris and Jacobs 1984). Researchers who study children's conceptual change—the changing of students' stored knowledge, or schemas, as they learn new things—have generally taken one of two perspectives on how children's knowledge is structured and how it changes with learning (diSessa 2006). Although these perspectives offer very different understandings of the way children acquire new knowledge, both of these perspectives have been (and continue to be) helpful in understanding how to teach children new knowledge that may add to, blend with, or replace their old knowledge (diSessa 2006). And, more important for our current discussion of struggling comprehenders, both of these perspectives provide useful insights into the nature of word callers' difficulties. For the purposes of our discussion, I will refer to one of these perspectives as the "theories" perspective and the other perspective as the "pieces" perspective.

The Theories Perspective

The theories perspective suggests that children's knowledge is well structured into organized, but naïve, theories about things they encounter in the world (Wellman and Gelman 1992). Sometimes these theories may be consistent with adult knowledge, such as when children believe that animal parents will have offspring that look like themselves (Springer and Keil 1989). And, as we discussed in the previous section, children develop theories of mind to help them understand how their own and others' minds work, and this enables them to interact more successfully in social situations (Astington, Harris, and Olson 1988). However, sometimes children's naïve theories lead them astray. For example, in the domain of physics knowledge, elementary-aged children believe that a ball rolling off a table will fall straight down to the floor rather than continuing its forward trajectory and landing a short distance from the table (Kaiser, Proffitt, and McCloskey 1985). If we apply the theories perspective to word callers' understanding of reading, we find that their naïve theories about reading may actually hinder, rather than help, their reading performance. Word callers typically believe that reading is about decoding processes, accuracy, and pronouncing words correctly (Gaskins and Gaskins 1997; Yuill and Oakhill 1991). These inaccurate (and incomplete) theories about reading may actually lead word callers to miss the purpose for reading, which is to gain meaning from text. And, as we learned in Chapter 1, because struggling readers tend to receive decoding-focused instruction rather than more meaning-focused instruction, these children's school experiences may not help them revise their theories about reading in ways that enable a more meaning-focused approach.

> **INSIGHT 2:** Word callers' theories about reading are inaccurate and incomplete. They believe the purpose of reading is fluent, accurate decoding, which leads them to focus on letter-sound information and not meaning.

The Pieces Perspective

The Theories Perspective suggested that children develop coherent theories, albeit naïve ones, that guide their understanding of various domains of knowledge. As I noted above, there is a second perspective on children's knowledge acquisition, the Pieces Perspective, which suggests, instead, that children tend to think about new information as isolated facts and do not necessarily make connections across different bits of knowledge within a domain (diSessa 2006; diSessa, Gillespie, and Esterly 2004). In other words, the Pieces Perspective suggests that children compartmentalize their knowledge and do not necessarily link different, related knowledge components together. Reading, of course, involves many different components (Adams 1990). If we apply the Pieces Perspective to word callers' thinking about reading, we find that these children may think about each of the important components of reading, such as meaning, letter-sound information, and syntax, as isolated from one another, and not integrate them while reading. I remember working with a particular second-grade boy who seemed to think about his reading knowledge in pieces. We were working on exercises designed to teach children how to think about sounds and meanings of printed words at the same time (Cartwright 2002, 2006). (This intervention will be described in Chapter 4.) In this particular instance, the student was supposed to be sorting words by sound and meaning, and he had only sorted by sound. When I corrected his mistake, he exclaimed, "Oh, it has to be a food, too! I just sorted it by how it sounded" (Cartwright 2006, 632). In a recent study of 155 second- to fifth-grade students who completed the sound-meaning sorting task I just described, I found that 30 percent of these students provided

> **INSIGHT 3:** Word callers think about the components of reading, such as letter-sound information, meaning, and syntax, as separate, distinct pieces of knowledge and, unlike skilled readers, do not spontaneously integrate them while reading.

sorts or explanations (for corrected sorts) that focused only on sound, without attention to meaning (Cartwright et al. 2009). Students like these come to the reading task thinking about each of the important components of reading separately, one kind of information at a time. Integrating multiple kinds of information while reading—that is, putting the pieces together—is difficult for these children, and their comprehension suffers as a result.

What Kinds of Mental Habits Are Necessary?

To illustrate this concept, consider a first grader, Derek (a pseudonym), who received one-to-one tutoring in the Reading Recovery program (Clay 1985, 1991, 2001) at his elementary school. During his first tutoring sessions, Derek's teacher, Mrs. Kent (also a pseudonym), had to remind him regularly to "Sit like a reader and keep your eyes on the book," because his attention would wander from the text on the table to many other spots around the reading resource room. Furthermore, when Derek would read aloud, he had a tendency to blurt out the first word that came to mind, based on partial information in a text, such as saying "The dog chased the boy down the start" for the sentence *The dog chased the boy down the street*.

Now consider the changes in Derek's reading behavior after several weeks of Reading Recovery tutoring. Derek has a newfound attentional focus: he no longer needs reminders to keep his eyes on the text. He now sits proudly "like a reader" as he focuses on his book and reads aloud. And, when he comes to a tricky word in text, such as *smelly* in the sentence *Sadie was smelly because she ran into a skunk in the woods*, he pauses and says "small, no, sm- smell-, smelly!" Then, he says, "I thought that was *small*, but I knew *small* didn't make sense, 'cause skunks can't make you small. Then I looked all the way through the word and saw the *e* and the *y*, and I figured out it was *smelly*. *Smelly* makes sense, 'cause skunks can make you smelly!"

When he first began Reading Recovery lessons, Derek seemed unable to direct his own thinking and reading processes. His attention wandered, and he was impulsive, apparently unable to inhibit his initial responses and engage in strategic, goal-directed thinking related to text. But, after some tutoring, Derek had much more control of his thinking. He had a goal: to understand a text. And, he was able to direct his attention to the reading task, inhibit his initial, impulsive response to the text, and engage in intentional problem solving to construct meaning. Not only that, but his comments indicated that he was aware of his goal and the problem solving he used to achieve it. In other words, Derek purposefully directed his own thinking to achieve the goal of reading for meaning.

Good Readers Guide Their Own Thinking

As this example illustrates, to be a successful reader (and to be successful at almost any task), children and adults must control their own thinking processes in particular ways. When we purposefully direct our thinking, we do so by using executive control processes: deliberate mental activities that help us achieve our goals (De Luca et al. 2003; Hughes 2002). These deliberate mental activities include such things as attention, inhibition, working memory, and cognitive flexibility (which will be described in the next section), and I describe each of these below.

- *Attention* involves the ability to direct one's focus to particular objects, information, or tasks. When Derek focused on the text he was reading (and was able to tune out other external distracters in the reading resource room), he was controlling his attention processes.

- *Inhibition* involves the ability to keep from responding in a certain way, and instead to think deliberately before providing a response. Children who blurt out answers in class without raising their hands or waiting to be called upon demonstrate a lack of inhibition. Similarly, when reading aloud, children show a lack of inhibition when they say the first word that comes to mind before they have fully analyzed a word in the text, such as when Derek mistakenly read *street* as *start* in his initial tutoring lesson. With respect to constructing meaning, the ability to discern relevant from irrelevant information in text and to inhibit responses to irrelevant information permits readers to carefully construct rich understandings of text without leaping to misleading conclusions. Not surprisingly, word callers have more difficulty suppressing irrelevant information when they read, which leads them to recall inappropriate, irrelevant facts from text, thus impairing their comprehension (De Beni and Palladino 2000; De Beni et al. 1998).

- Finally, *working memory* involves the ability to hold several things in mind while using part of them (Bayliss et al. 2005). For example, when a child is writing in her journal and looks at the word wall to check a spelling, she must retain all of the letters in that word in her working memory while she writes each individual letter, one at a time, in her journal. Essentially, working memory can be thought of as the amount of mental space one has to store and consciously work on information, which implicates two general kinds of processes: relatively passive, mental storage operations and relatively conscious, active operations.

Working memory is related to reading comprehension in both good and poor comprehenders, and it varies in both groups of children (Cain, Oakhill, and Bryant 2004; Oakhill, Hartt, and Samols 2005). And, as we learned in Chapter 1, word callers seem to be equivalent to better comprehenders on more passive, storage-related measures of working memory (Oakhill, Yuill, and Parkin 1986; Stothard and Hulme 1992). However, on more complex, active working memory assessments, such as detecting text inconsistencies that are separated by distance (Oakhill, Hartt, and Samols 2005; Yuill, Oakhill, and Parkin 1989), word callers do more poorly than their peers with better comprehension. (See Cain and Oakhill 2007 for a discussion of working memory in poor comprehenders.)

Although there is some debate, many researchers (including myself) believe that working memory is separable from—though certainly related to—other executive processes like inhibition, cognitive flexibility, and attentional control, especially in children (Garon, Bryson, and Smith 2008; Guajardo, Parker, and Turley-Ames 2009; Kane et al. 2006; Unsworth and Engle 2008). Thus, differences between word callers and more skilled comprehenders on more complex, active working memory tasks may actually reflect differences in other, specific executive processes, such as inhibition or cognitive flexibility. As you will see in the next section, cognitive flexibility may be a good candidate for study and intervention with these struggling readers.

Any discussion of working memory and reading would be remiss if it did not mention the role of automatic decoding in freeing mental space (i.e., working memory) for comprehension. For many years we have assumed that if decoding processes are automatic, enough mental space would be freed to support comprehension (LaBerge and Samuels 1974; Samuels 2002). Fluency is certainly related to comprehension for most students (Kuhn and Stahl 2003; Laberge and Samuels 1974; National Reading Panel 2000; Samuels 2002). However, as we learned in Chapter 1, there are many children (about a third of our struggling readers) who are able to decode fluently—and automatically—yet still do not comprehend text. Thus, simply freeing mental space is not sufficient to ensure comprehension. Our discussion of cognitive flexibility in the next section may shed some light on why this is the case.

These kinds of deliberate mental activities—attention, inhibition, and working memory—develop across childhood (De Luca et al. 2003), and they play an important role in academic tasks (Blair and Razza 2007; Reiter, Tucha, and Lange 2004; St Clair-Thompson and Gathercole 2006) because they enable children to exert control over their own thinking. And, although word callers are similar to their peers on some measures of working memory (Oakhill, Yuill, and Parkin 1986), they are less able to deliberately direct their reading-related mental activities in other ways. For example, they monitor (or pay attention to) their own comprehension less, they are less aware of the effectiveness of reading strategies, and they are less adept at deliberately adapting monitoring skills to repair their comprehension when it fails (August, Flavell, and Clift 1984). With respect to goal-directed mental activities, word callers adopt different goals than their peers with better comprehension, focusing on getting words right, not getting meaning (Paris and Myers 1981).

> **INSIGHT 4:** Word callers have more difficulty engaging in deliberate, goal-directed mental activities—executive processes—that support skilled reading than their peers with better comprehension. Even when engaging in deliberate, goal-directed reading behavior, word callers' goals do not support comprehension because they focus on decoding rather than on getting meaning from text. Because children naturally vary in executive processes, word callers' difficulties in this area may simply be due to natural developmental variation. However, because teachers tend to engage in more decoding-focused instruction with struggling readers (Allington 1980; Chinn et al. 1993; also see Mertzman 2008), we cannot rule out the effects of prior instruction on these children's processes.

How We Can Help These Children Learn

Any teacher of reading will attest that reading is tremendously complex (Adams 1990). As you read this text, for example, you are seamlessly integrating many features, such as your knowledge of word meanings, letter-sound knowledge, syntactic information, and your prior knowledge of reading processes. And, while managing the integration of all of these features, you are also monitoring your own comprehension and using strategies to improve or repair your comprehension when necessary.

Early in the chapter we learned that children develop the ability to hold more than one idea in mind at once (as depicted in Figure 2–1), which is certainly necessary for handling the many kinds of information required for skilled reading. Often, however, when we engage in complex tasks we must do much more than simply hold multiple features in mind while working on some of them. We must actively switch between those features. This mental switching is another aspect of executive control, called *cognitive flexibility,* which enables children (and adults) to actively go between multiple ideas when engaging in tasks. Michael Pressley and his colleagues aptly described this flexible switching as "cognitive juggling" (Pressley et al. 2008). Just as we might physically juggle several objects at once, adeptly switching between them as we toss them into the air, cognitive flexibility involves switching between mental "objects."

Cognitive flexibility improves with age (Davidson et al. 2006; De Luca et al. 2003) and develops more slowly than other executive functions, such as inhibition and working memory (De Luca et al. 2003). Thus, it should come as no surprise that cognitive flexibility varies widely, with some children performing better than adults (Cartwright et al. 2006; Kuhn and Pease 2006). Most important for our discussion, the ability to think flexibly about the components of reading tasks, such as sounds and meanings of printed words, is important to reading comprehension in children (Cartwright 2002; Cartwright et al. 2010) and adults (Cartwright 2007). And, as you might expect, word callers are significantly less able to think flexibly about sounds and meanings of printed words than their peers with better comprehension (Cartwright and Coppage 2009; Cartwright et al. 2008). My colleagues and I have found that flexible thinking can be taught to second- to fifth-grade students, resulting in improved cognitive flexibility and reading comprehension. And good news for the busy classroom teacher, the consummate juggler: the improvement can occur in only five lessons (Chapter 4 describes this intervention; Cartwright 2002; Cartwright, Clause, and Schmidt 2007). Cognitive flexibility is probably the most complex thinking process we have discussed thus far because it involves the processes reviewed earlier in the chapter: the ability to think about multiple ideas at once, the understanding that reading involves more components than letter-sound information, the ability to integrate various pieces of information while reading, and the ability to purposefully direct one's own thought processes.

> **INSIGHT 5:** Word callers' thinking is less flexible than their peers', with better comprehension. In particular, they have difficulty actively switching between the many important components that must be coordinated for skilled reading.

Closing Notes

New work on children's thinking yields several important insights that help us understand word callers' difficulties with comprehension. In particular, word callers

- have difficulty thinking about more than one idea at a time
- have incomplete theories of reading that lead them to miss the purpose for reading
- have difficulty integrating the several important components of reading tasks
- have difficulty purposefully directing their own thinking processes, and
- are less cognitively flexible than their peers with better comprehension.

In the remaining chapters of the book I will present a research-based assessment of flexible thinking that you can use in your classroom to gauge how flexible your own students are at thinking about both sounds and meanings of words. After that, I will offer several research-based strategies that have been used successfully to target particular aspects of word callers' difficulties. Finally, in the last chapter I will share an instructional approach that is effective in helping word callers understand the active, strategic nature of good comprehenders' thinking. As I present each of these instructional strategies and approaches, I will return to the concepts discussed in this chapter to anchor the practice in research on children's thinking and to illustrate how the strategy improves word callers' comprehension.

How Does This Help You?

Questions to Consider

- Have you observed instances in which your students have difficulty considering multiple ideas or perspectives? What practices might help students step outside their own views?

- Ask your students what good readers do. Their answers may surprise you. What do their responses reveal about their understanding of the "goal" of reading? How might their goals affect their approaches to texts?

- When your students exhibit reading difficulties, consider the flexibility (or inflexibility) of their thinking. What elements do they notice in the text, and what do they miss? How might you help them integrate these elements for better reading?

3

Who Are Your Inflexible Thinkers?

A Quick Classroom Assessment*

Imagine a third grader, Brittany (a fictitious but representative student), who is sitting across from me one afternoon at a quiet table in her classroom. I am a researcher visiting Brittany's school to study the role of flexible thinking in reading comprehension, and Brittany is excited to leave her regular classroom activities to play "reading games" with me. We are looking at some cards with printed words, such as the words in Figure 3–1, which can be sorted by initial sound and word meaning to assess Brittany's flexible thinking about print. For all intents and purposes, Brittany appears to be a typical student. She is bright and engaged. She decodes fluently. However, she struggles with comprehension.

FIGURE 3–1

A Set of Sound-Meaning Sort Words

bear	bunny	bird
boat	bus	bike
tiger	turkey	toad
train	truck	tractor

After demonstrating a 2 × 2 sort with a different set of words, I ask Brittany to sort the words in Figure 3–1 in two ways, just like I showed her: by how the words sound and by what the words mean. As you might imagine after reading the list, the words can be sorted into four piles of three cards each, divided according to sound (/b/ or /t/) and meaning (vehicles or animals). See Figure 3–2 for a correct sort of these cards, which divides them by sound and meaning along the columns and rows of the matrix, respectively.

Well, even though I have just shown Brittany how to do the 2 × 2 sort, and even though I explain that she should sort two ways, just like I showed her, Brittany sorts the cards into only two piles: a pile of words that start with the /b/ sound and a pile of words that start with the /t/ sound (see Figure 3–3). When I correct her sort (so that it looks like Figure 3–2) and ask her

*Coauthored with Elizabeth A. Coppage

"Why do you think we would sort them this way?," Brittany seems to experience a flash of insight, exclaiming, "Oh! I just did the sounds. I have to think about whether they're animals or transportation, too!"

FIGURE 3–2

A Correct Sort of the Sound-Meaning Sort Words in Figure 3–1

FIGURE 3–3

Brittany's Sort of the Sound-Meaning Sort Words in Figure 3–1

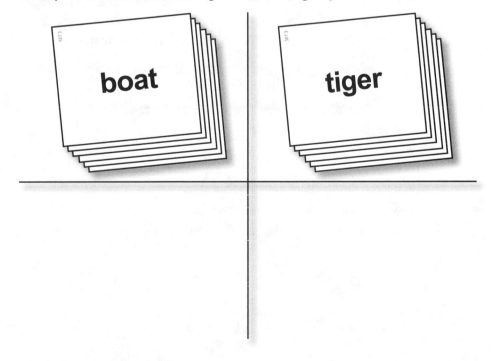

This opening vignette illustrates the inflexibility we typically see in word callers' thinking. These children are less able to hold words' sounds and meanings in mind at once and flexibly switch between them. Not surprisingly, in a recent study comparing word callers to skilled comprehenders, word callers performed significantly more poorly on this assessment than their peers with better comprehension (Cartwright and Coppage 2009). Like these children, Brittany performed poorly on this assessment, focusing solely on sound for her sort. When I showed her a correct sort, she had an "aha!" moment because she realized that meaning was important, too; she also realized that she had not been thinking about it. This is the first step on the way to learning how to deliberately consider both sounds and meanings while reading. (I should note that children may also demonstrate inflexible thinking on these sorts by focusing only on meaning and not on sounds. In these cases, too, children demonstrate an inability to coordinate multiple components that are important for skilled reading.)

Who Are Your Inflexible Thinkers?
An Assessment to Try

Now I'd like to share a cognitive flexibility assessment I developed, which you can use to determine the degree to which your students can think flexibly about sounds and meanings of printed words (Cartwright 2002, 2006, 2007, 2008c; Cartwright et al. 2006; Cartwright, Isaac, and Dandy 2006). In this chapter I provide step-by-step instructions for performing the brief (5–10 minutes) flexible thinking assessment, the reproducible worksheet necessary for scoring the assessment, and average scores for strong readers and word callers across grade levels for comparison purposes, so that you know what to expect from your students. Finally, the materials you need to conduct the assessment accompany the book and can also be used to teach flexible thinking (a process described in Chapter 4), which improves reading comprehension. The ability to assess students' flexible thinking about words' sounds and meanings offers the opportunity to

- explain the inflexibility you might have observed in your students, which may contribute to their comprehension difficulties

- determine which of your students might benefit from additional exercises to improve flexible thinking, and thus comprehension

- measure your students' flexible thinking before and after you administer interventions (or at the beginning and end of marking periods) to assess whether your students' flexible thinking has changed, and

- improve flexible thinking about print, using the assessment materials for a flexible thinking intervention, which is described in Chapter 4.

INSIGHT FROM CHILDREN'S THINKING

Reading requires flexible attention to many aspects of texts, but word callers are typically less cognitively flexible than their peers. This flexible thinking assessment enables teachers to determine whether students can consider flexibly both sounds and meanings of print, providing important diagnostic information to inform instruction for struggling students.

The Research Base

As we learned in Chapter 2, research findings on children's thinking from fields in the Learning Sciences, such as cognitive development, neuroscience, and educational psychology, has focused on executive control processes, or those deliberate goal-directed mental activities that support academic tasks, like reading. Struggling comprehenders' difficulty with understanding what they read may sometimes be explained in terms of a particular executive control process, cognitive flexibility, which is the ability to consider multiple aspects of a task at once and mentally switch between those task features (Cartwright et al. 2010; Jacques and Zelazo 2005). Sorting tasks are particularly well suited to assessing cognitive flexibility because they enable us to see easily whether children can switch between multiple aspects of the sorted objects (Inhelder and Piaget 1964; Jacques and Zelazo 2005). Some of these tasks require children to sort along one dimension, say color, and then switch the sorting rule and sort by shape (e.g., the Dimensional Change Card Sort, Zelazo et al. 2003), whereas other tasks have children sort by multiple dimensions at once (e.g., the multiple classification task, Bigler and Liben 1992; Cartwright 2002; Inhelder and Piaget 1964). And, although many researchers have found relations between general assessments of cognitive flexibility (such as thinking flexibly about colors and shapes of objects) and reading ability (e.g., Arlin 1981; Briggs and Elkind 1973; Cohen, Hyman, and Battistini 1983; Reiter, Tucha, and Lange 2004), their work didn't tell us exactly how cognitive flexibility might be related to reading.

I wondered whether we might be able to assess flexibility in thinking about *specific* aspects of reading, and I created the sorting task with which I opened the chapter, adapted from other work in cognitive development (Bigler and Liben 1992; Inhelder and Piaget 1964). This task requires children (or adults) to sort words by sound and meaning simultaneously, to assess the degree to which they can think flexibly about these particular components of print (Cartwright 2002). Sound-meaning flexibility (also called graphophonological-semantic cognitive flexibility) contributes to reading comprehension in beginning readers (Cartwright et al. 2010), second to fourth graders (Cartwright 2002), and adults. As you might expect, sound-meaning flexibility improves across the lifespan, and it varies within grade levels, with some children performing better than some adults (Cartwright, Isaac, and Dandy 2006). More important for our discussion, at-risk readers are about half as flexible as their typically developing peers (Cartwright 2008c), and as noted above, word callers are less than half as flexible as good comprehenders (Cartwright and Coppage 2009). This kind of reading-specific cognitive flexibility has particular relevance for teachers, as it can be taught, resulting in improvements in reading comprehension (Cartwright 2002, 2006; Cartwright, Clause, and Schmidt 2007). The exercises used to teach it will be described in Chapter 4.

Giving the Assessment: Materials, Steps, Scoring Tips

This quick assessment provides a way to determine how well readers can think about two aspects of print (sound and meaning) at the same time. The assessment is administered individually and takes approximately 5 to 10 minutes for most students. During the assessment, you will model the sound-meaning sort with one set of words, and then students will sort four sets of printed words by sound and meaning at the same time into a 2 × 2 matrix, just like the cards in Figure 3–2. Correct sorts force students to think beyond sounds and also focus on meaning. Thus, the assessment provides an index of their ability to think about both features at once and flexibly switch between them.

Materials

To perform the assessment, you will need the following materials. Although nine sets of word cards and the 2 × 2 matrix accompany the book, you will only need five sets of word cards for the assessment. (See Figure 3–4 for lists of words in each of the sets.) The four extra word sets can be used for posttesting your students at a later time.

- five sets of twelve word cards (one to teach the task, four to assess the student)
- 2 × 2 matrix
- stopwatch
- Assessment Scoring Sheet (see Figure 3–5 for the reproducible sheet)
- a clipboard (to hold the scoring sheet in your lap, out of the student's view)
- a pencil or pen to record scores

FIGURE 3–4

Word Card Sets		
Set 1	/k/ and /p/: foods and school supplies	cake, corn, carrot, calendar, clip, crayon, peach, peas, plum, pencil, pen, paper
Set 2	/ch/ and /h/: body parts and food	cheek, chest, chin, chips, cheese, chicken, hair, hand, head, ham, honey, hot dog
Set 3	/b/ and /t/: vehicles and animals	bike, boat, bus, bunny, bear, bird, tractor, train, truck, tiger, toad, turkey
Set 4	/k/ and /b/: containers and foods	crate, can, cup, carrot, corn, cookie, basket, box, bag, beans, banana, butter
Set 5	/f/ and /t/: body parts and animals	foot, face, finger, fish, fox, frog, tummy, toes, tooth, toad, turtle, tiger
Set 6	/k/ and /sh/: actions and clothes	cry, call, crawl, cape, cap, coat, shake, shout, shove, shorts, shoe, shirt
Set 7	/d/ and /p/: animals and people	deer, dog, donkey, dancer, dentist, doctor, panda, pig, puppy, pilot, pirate, president
Set 8	/b/ and /s/: food and clothes	banana, beans, bread, belt, bonnet, boot, salad, soup, stew, skirt, sock, sweater
Set 9	/f/ and /d/: animals and actions	dog, duck, deer, fawn, foal, fox, draw, dig, dance, fuss, fix, find

FIGURE 3–5

Sound-Meaning Flexible Thinking Assessment Scoring Sheet

STUDENT NAME: _____ DATE: _____ GRADE: _____

Set A _____   Time: _____ sec.

sort   Y   N   Points: _____

explanation   Y   N

Set B _____   Time: _____ sec.

sort   Y   N   Points: _____

explanation   Y   N

Set C _____   Time: _____ sec.

sort   Y   N   Points: _____

explanation   Y   N

Set D _____   Time: _____ sec.

sort   Y   N   Points: _____

explanation   Y   N

Computing the Flexible Thinking Score

(Total Accuracy/Average Sort Time × 100)

Total Accuracy = _____ + _____ + _____ + _____   =   ☐

                 Set A Points Set B Points Set C Points Set D Points

Average Sort Time = _____ + _____ + _____ + _____ / 4 =   ☐

                    Set A Time Set B Time Set C Time Set D Time

× 100

Notes About Explanations:
- MUST focus on two dimensions
- CANNOT focus on one cell at a time

Points for Scoring

0 = neither correct
1 = sort only correct
2 = explanation only correct
3 = both correct

Total Score = ☐

Directions

Find a quiet desk or table where you can sit with your student, and place the 2 × 2 matrix on the table in front of the student.

Teach the Sound-Meaning Sort

Select one set of cards to demonstrate the task, and set aside four additional sets to assess your student.

- Introduce the task by saying, "I have some cards for you to sort, and you can sort these cards two ways at the same time. See, you can sort these cards by how they sound and by what they mean. Here, let me show you."

- Sort the cards, one at a time, into the 2 × 2 matrix so that they are sorted by sound along one axis (rows or columns) and by meaning along the other. You should have four piles of three cards, with a pile in each quadrant of the matrix. (Note: The words must be sorted by how they sound and what they mean simultaneously, and diagonal sorts are not permitted. See Figure 3–2 for an example.)

- Explain your sort to the student, while pointing to the rows and columns in the matrix. Make sure that you focus on rows and columns in your explanation, not on individual piles, so that students clearly understand the 2 × 2 nature of the sort. Explanations that focus on individual piles lead students to think about individual features of the words (promoting inflexible thinking). For the cards in Figure 3–2, you might say

    "I put all the vehicles up here" (while pointing to the top row)

    "I put all the animals down here" (while pointing to the bottom row)

    "I put all the /b/ words on this side" (while pointing to the left column)

    "And, I put all the /t/ words over here" (while pointing to the right column)

Assess Your Student

You will need the Assessment Scoring Sheet, a clipboard, a pencil or pen, a stopwatch, and four new sets of word cards to assess your student. Record the word sets you choose for the assessment on the scoring sheet in the blanks provided (Figure 3–5; see Figure 3–6, on page 32, for an example). You will record your student's sort time for each set of cards, whether your student sorts each set correctly, and whether your student explains each sort correctly.

- Position your scoring sheet so that your student can't see it. (Holding it on a clipboard in your lap may help with this.)

- Ensure your stopwatch is ready to time your student's sort. (Although you are timing, be aware that students are permitted to have as much time as necessary to complete the sorts.)

- Tell your student, "Now I have some cards for you to sort, and you can sort these cards two ways at the same time, just like I showed you. I'm going to time you, just to see how long it takes, but you don't have to hurry. If you don't know a word, it's okay. I can help you."

- Hand the student the first set of twelve word cards, and start timing the sort when the student looks at the first card. Stop timing when the student places the last card in the matrix. Record the sort time in seconds in the blank for that set on the Assessment Scoring Sheet.

- If the student does not know a word (either how to pronounce it or what it means), you may read it for the student or explain the meaning (e.g., "A bonnet is a kind of hat"). The sorting task is intended to be an assessment of flexible thinking, not an assessment of decoding or vocabulary knowledge. Providing missing word knowledge enables us to assess flexible thinking.

- If the student sorts all of the cards correctly, circle "Y" on the scoring sheet for that set, and ask the child, "Why did you sort them that way?"

- If the student sorts incorrectly (even if the student misplaces only one card or sorts diagonally), circle "N" on the scoring sheet for that set, and re-sort the cards so that they are sorted correctly. Then, ask the student, "Why do you think we would sort them that way?"

- The student's explanation for the correct sort should focus on both dimensions of the sort and not on each pile of cards individually. For example, a correct explanation might look like this, with the student pointing to the appropriate rows and columns: "I put the /b/ words over here and the /t/ words over here, and I put the animals down here and the things-that-go up here."

If the student's explanation refers to only one dimension (e.g., "I sorted by /b/ words and /t/ words"), you may prompt once with the question, "Anything else?" A correct response to this question would refer to the missing dimension of the sort (e.g., "Oh, I sorted by meaning, too: vehicles and animals").

Some students' explanations focus on one pile of cards at a time, rather than on the two sorting dimensions, indicating a focus on single elements of the sort (and less flexible thinking). For example, the student might point to each pile individually and say, "I put the animals that start with /b/ here, I put the animals that start with /t/ here, I put the vehicles that start with /b/ here, and I put the vehicles that start with /t/ here." Students who offer these explanations may not be able to focus on the two complete sorting dimensions at once. In these cases, you should prompt with the question, "What two ways did you sort them?" A correct response to this question would refer to the complete sound and meaning dimensions: "I sorted by sound: /b/ and /t/, and I sorted by meaning: animals and vehicles."

- Circle "Y" for a correct explanation that focuses on both sorting dimensions (sound and meaning) and "N" for an incorrect explanation.

Repeat these steps for three additional card sets, recording the student's responses as you go.

Record the Scores for Each Set

Students with the highest levels of cognitive flexibility sort more quickly, they sort accurately, and they provide explanations that focus on both dimensions. So, scoring involves all three components: sorting time, correctness of the sorts, and correctness of the explanations. Sorting time should be recorded in seconds for each card set.

Students receive points for accuracy of sorts and explanations. Points are allocated for each card set according to a rubric that privileges correct explanations over correct sorts without the ability to explain them. The rubric for allocating those points can be found at the bottom of the Assessment Scoring Sheet. The following sort-explanation response combinations yield points for each set as follows:

- Y and Y: Students receive 3 points for each card set with a correct sort and explanation.

- N and Y: Students receive 2 points for each card set that they sort incorrectly (i.e., anything less than 100 percent correct) but for which they give a correct explanation for the teacher-corrected sort. (Typically, students who are able to provide an appropriate explanation for a corrected sort have misplaced only one or two cards, or they sort diagonally, which is not permitted on the task.)

- Y and N: Students receive one point for a correct sort and incorrect verbal explanation, indicating little explicit awareness of the multidimensional nature of the task.

- N and N: Students receive no points when both the sort and explanation are incorrect.

In sum, students can earn up to 12 points for the correctness of their sorts and explanations across the four card sets (following Bigler and Liben 1992; Cartwright 2002, 2007; Cartwright, Isaac, and Dandy 2006; Cartwright et al. 2010; Golbeck 1983). This scoring scheme for sorting accuracy reflects the usual course of cognitive development, as children typically are able to perform a task before they are able to verbally articulate the reasons for their performance (Flavell, Miller, and Miller 2002; Inhelder and Piaget 1964).

Calculate a Total Score

The formula for calculating your student's sound-meaning flexible thinking score is at the bottom of the Assessment Scoring Sheet (see Figure 3–5). The total score includes information on your student's accuracy and his or her sorting speed. Just transfer the scores for individual card sets to the appropriate blanks at the bottom of the scoring sheet (sorting time in seconds, and the points earned for each card set). See Figure 3–6 for an example of how to calculate a score. Then, add the points earned across the four card sets to yield a sum that can range from 0 to 12. This number should be recorded in the top box: the numerator. Next, add the four sorting times together and divide by 4 to get an average sorting time. Record this in the next box: the denominator. Finally, divide the points by the average sorting time, and multiply by 100, and record the result in the bottom box. This number is your total score. See the sample worksheet in Figure 3–6.

FIGURE 3–6

Brittany's Score on the Sound-Meaning Flexible Thinking Assessment

Sound-Meaning Flexible Thinking Assessment Scoring Sheet

STUDENT NAME: _Brittany_____ DATE: _6/1___ GRADE: _4___

Set A _/b/ and /t/; vehicles and animals_____

sort   Y   (N)

explanation   (Y)   N

Time: _72.56_ sec.

Points: _2___

Set B _/ch/ and /w/; body parts and food_____

sort   Y   (N)

explanation   Y   (N)

Time: _65.32_ sec.

Points: _0___

Set C _/k/ and /b/; containers and foods_____

sort   (Y)   N

explanation   (Y)   N

Time: _47.21_ sec.

Points: _3___

Set D _/f/ and /t/; body parts and animals_____

sort   (Y)   N

explanation   Y   (N)

Time: _51.78_ sec.

Points: _1___

Computing the Flexible Thinking Score

(Total Accuracy/Average Sort Time × 100)

Total Accuracy = ____2____ + ____0____ + ____3____ + ____1____ =   6

             Set A Points   Set B Points   Set C Points   Set D Points

Average Sort Time = __72.56__ + __65.32__ + __47.21__ + __51.78__ / 4 =   59.22

                 Set A Time   Set B Time   Set C Time   Set D Time

× 100

Notes About Explanations:
- MUST focus on two dimensions
- CANNOT focus on one cell at a time

Points for Scoring

0 = neither correct
1 = sort only correct
2 = explanation only correct
3 = both correct

Total Score =   10.13

Compare the total score to the scores in Figure 3–7 to see how your student's performance compares to the performance of students I have tested in my work. The chart in Figure 3–7 provides scores for typical good readers and for word callers across elementary grade levels. I also included scores for college students to give you a perspective on how young adults might perform on the task. If we compare Brittany's score to the chart in Figure 3–7, we find that her sound-meaning flexible thinking is below average for her grade level. Given that Brittany is low in sound-meaning flexibility, and given that she focused only on sound in her initial sort (described at the beginning of this chapter), Brittany might benefit from some of the techniques described in Chapters 4 to 8 of this book to improve her focus on meaning.

FIGURE 3–7

Sound-Meaning Flexible Thinking Scores Across Grades for Strong Readers and Word Callers

Grade	Strong Readers			Word Callers		
	Average Score	Range (Low & High Scores)		Average Score	Range (Low & High Scores)	
1st	9.80	o	24.68	3.51	o	7.96
2nd	12.38	o	33.90	4.86	o	28.69
3rd	13.17	o	46.06	7.49	o	20.68
4th	16.67	o	42.91	9.08	o	33.58
5th	22.55	o	53.71	12.42	2.79	19.60
College	53.69	16.77	100.25	44.69	5.49	75.85

Answers to Teachers' Frequently Asked Questions

As a classroom teacher or reading specialist trying this assessment for the first time, you may have some questions about how it might work with your students in your classroom. In this section I provide a few of the most common questions I have received about this assessment, along with answers, to help you get started.

Q: To whom should I administer this assessment? Should I assess all of the students in my class?

A: Because children within each grade level (and even adults) vary on this assessment, it may provide useful information about individual students' processing that you can use to plan your instruction. For example, you may find that some of your students have difficulty coordinating words' sounds and meanings, other students may focus only on meanings, and still other students may focus on words' sounds. Each of these patterns tells you a bit about your students' thinking and can help you determine whether your students need additional instructional support to help them process and coordinate particular aspects of print.

Q: Can I administer the assessment in small groups?

A: No, this is an individual assessment. You must time each student's sorting, and the student must provide explanations for correct (or corrected) sorts. These are best accomplished in a one-to-one format so that you can accurately assess each individual student's level of flexible thinking.

Q: What if my student cannot read the words on the cards?

A: A basic assumption underlying this assessment is that students have at least a moderate level of decoding skills because we want the assessment to measure flexible thinking—not whether a student can decode words. If your student has a great deal of trouble decoding the words for the assessment, then his or her reading difficulties probably extend beyond comprehension, and that child's scores will likely be significantly affected by decoding difficulties. In these cases, students may need more decoding work before they are ready to work on flexible thinking. Occasionally, students might have trouble with a word here or there, despite adequate decoding skill, and in these cases, you should provide the correct pronunciation (or meaning) for the student. (For example, I have had students ask me what a *bonnet* is, and I tell them, "It's a kind of hat.") When you introduce the assessment you should remember to tell your student, "If you don't know a word, it's okay. I can help you," so that your student knows to ask for help when needed.

Q: When should I administer this assessment of flexible thinking?

A: You could test your students' flexible thinking at the beginning of the school year to see where they are in relation to one another and in relation to other children who have been tested (see Figure 3–7). This beginning-of-year assessment will help you determine whether your students are able to coordinate flexibly the sounds and meanings of print and may help you determine which students might benefit from exercises designed to increase their flexible thinking to improve comprehension (Chapter 4). Assessment results might help you choose which students to include in small-group flexible thinking lessons (see Chapter 4). You might also decide to repeat the assessment at later points in the school year, especially after flexible thinking and/or comprehension interventions, to determine whether your students' flexible thinking has improved. Another way you might consider using the assessment is as a targeted diagnostic tool when you believe some of your students are particularly inflexible thinkers about print. The assessment will help you determine, for example, whether students are sound-focused, like typical word callers, in which case they might need additional, targeted lessons to improve their focus on sounds and meaning simultaneously.

Q: How do I incorporate this assessment into the school day?

A: You might train a teacher's aide to administer the assessment while you are working with small groups during your language arts block, or you might test individual children while the rest of the class is at literacy centers. Another option is to work with your reading specialist who can pull students out of class to perform the assessment.

Q: I gave the instructions for the assessment and modeled a correct sort and explanation for my student, just as the directions suggested. But, my student doesn't seem to get the task. What should I do? Can I repeat the directions?

A: In the research on flexible thinking, we did not repeat the directions for students because this would have given some students extra support that other students did not have. The scores in Figure 3–7 are based on assessments with directions that match those described in this chapter. If we were to provide extra support by repeating directions for some students and not others, we would not be able to compare results meaningfully across children, and comparisons to the scores in Figure 3–7 would also lose their meaning. If your student seems stuck, encourage her by saying something like, "Just sort them two ways like I showed you, by how they sound and what they mean. Do your best!" Remember, during the assessment students sort four different sets of cards, one set at a time, and the assessment process itself provides formative feedback for the students. If your student sorts incorrectly, you will correct the sort and then ask her for an explanation for your corrected sort (e.g., why would we sort them that way?), and this process often helps students understand the nature of the task because they see how a correct sort looks. Usually, across the four card sets in the assessment, students will improve from the first set to the last. Remember, too, that children at all elementary grade levels, first through fifth, have received scores of zero on this assessment, indicating very limited flexibility. So, variation in student ability is to be expected.

Q: My student wants to know how she did on the assessment. What do I tell her?

A: Just as you would with any assessment, offer encouragement and motivation and praise your student's efforts on the task without revealing details of her performance (e.g., "You worked really hard and did a great job!"). With this assessment, we genuinely want to know how students think about print to provide us useful diagnostic information about their cognitive flexibility. So, in that sense, there are no right answers, only interesting ones.

Q: My students want to spread out the cards on the table or look at them all in their hands before they put them in the matrix. Is this allowed?

A: Yes, your students are permitted to look at the cards in any way they choose, but you should not do so when you model the sort. When you model the sort, you should hold the stack of cards in your hand and place them, one card at a time, into four neat stacks (of three cards each) in the 2 × 2 matrix. When you give your students each set of cards for the assessment, remember that timing of each sort begins when your student *looks* at the first card in his or her hand (because that indicates the point at which your student begins thinking about the cards) and ends when the last card is placed in the matrix. Once you begin timing, your student can spread the cards out on the table, look through all the cards in her hand, or arrange and rearrange them in the matrix, if needed. You should not prompt these activities, but you should allow them if the student chooses them. Your student's sorting time will include all the time spent thinking about the cards until sorting is complete.

Q: **Why do I have so many word sets in the materials that accompany the book?**

A: We gave you multiple sets so that you would have enough word sets to pretest and posttest your students at different points during the school year, perhaps before and after an intervention or at the beginning and end of a marking period. You have nine sets. Choose one (perhaps the first set) to be your demonstration set. Then, the remaining eight sets can be used to assess students, four at pretest and four at posttest. Use the same demonstration set to model correct sorts and explanations both times. New sets are provided for posttest in order to ensure that students aren't improving in flexibility simply because they are using familiar words.

Q: **This task seems so different from reading real texts that I am skeptical about the relation between it and reading comprehension. Are they related, and how does this skill transfer to students' reading comprehension?**

A: The ability to think flexibly about sounds and meanings of print (measured with the assessment presented in this chapter) is significantly related to reading comprehension across the lifespan: in beginning readers (with a correlation of 0.61, Cartwright et al. 2010), in second to fourth graders (with a correlation of 0.70, Cartwright 2002), and in adults (with a correlation of 0.58, Cartwright 2007). Think about sound-meaning flexible thinking as a skill that *enables* comprehension rather than a skill that *transfers to* comprehension. The ability to think flexibly about the many aspects of print helps students to shift attention from words to meaning. Readers who can easily and flexibly consider meaning alongside letter-sound information will be better able to construct rich meanings while reading. However, readers who cannot think flexibly about both letter-sound information and meaning will be limited in their ability to derive meaning from text.

How Does This Help You?

Questions to Consider

- Do you have students now whom you think might have difficulty with this assessment? Why do you think so?

- At what points in the academic year would it be useful to assess your students' flexible thinking?

- How might flexible thinking assessment results affect your instruction: individual, small-group, or whole-group?

Easy Intervention Lessons
Word and Picture Sorts

4

In the last chapter you learned how to assess flexible thinking in your students, using the materials that accompany this
book; and, you met a student named Brittany who was fairly
inflexible in her approach to print. Rather than considering both
sounds and meanings of words, Brittany's initial inclination was
to focus on sounds alone, and the results of her flexible thinking
assessment indicated that she was less adept at thinking flexibly about sounds and meanings of words than other children
at her grade level (see Chapter 3). Fortunately for students like
Brittany, flexible thinking can be taught using the materials that
accompany this book, resulting in improvements in flexible
thinking and reading comprehension.

Skilled reading requires that we handle many, many text features at once, such as sounds and meaning, switching between
them as we process a text (Adams 1990; Cartwright 2008b).
Word callers in particular have difficulty considering sounds and
meanings at the same time, and, not surprisingly, they exhibit
less cognitive flexibility than good comprehenders (Cartwright
and Coppage 2009; Cartwright et al. 2008). The purpose of
this chapter is to share an intervention with you that I developed based on what we know about children's thinking. This
intervention improves students' ability to think flexibly about
words' sounds and meanings, whether delivered in one-to-one
or small-group formats, resulting in improved reading comprehension—in just five lessons (Cartwright 2002, 2006; Cartwright,
Clause, and Schmidt 2007).

The key to the intervention is that it requires children to think about both sounds and meanings at once, rather than thinking about each component independently. Although effective literacy teachers routinely integrate attention to words' sounds and meanings in texts (Pressley 2006a), students may not always integrate these features as easily as we would like. When we teach phonics skills, for example, students may focus primarily on the sounds of words. When we teach comprehension strategies, on the other hand, students may focus on meaning without attention to sound. This "single element" focus may not help our children learn to juggle all the features of print necessary for skilled reading. However, by forcing students to think about both sounds and meanings at once, and providing appropriate support and practice for this new skill, the sound-meaning flexible thinking intervention helps students to unglue from print (Chall 1996), changing the way they think about print and thus improving their comprehension. An example may help illustrate this point. Remember Derek, who we met in Chapter 2? Before he began Reading Recovery lessons, he was rather inflexible in his approach to print, and he misread the word *street*, pronouncing it *start* in the sentence *The dog chased the boy down the street*. Derek's mistake indicates that he was not using all of the letter-sound information available to him, but he did use most of it: *street* and *start* share all but one phoneme. What Derek's reading behavior may also indicate is that he was not attending to meaning. Had he been thinking about meaning in addition to letter-sound information, he would have noticed that *start* did not make sense in that context. Inflexible reading is evident when readers do not notice meaning—both appropriately constructed meanings and breakdowns in meaning construction. This behavior is typical of word callers, but it is also evident in beginning readers who are still mastering decoding processes. Flexible thinking exercises can help children shift attention to meaning, whether word callers or typical readers who need an extra nudge to focus on meaning. And, readers who focus on meanings without attention to words' sounds can also benefit from this intervention. This chapter will include directions and scoring sheets for the flexible thinking intervention; the materials you need for the one-to-one intervention accompany the book.

INSIGHT FROM CHILDREN'S THINKING

Successful readers are able to juggle mentally many elements of texts and actively switch between them while reading. This mental juggling, called cognitive flexibility, is an important aspect of children's deliberate goal-directed thinking, which helps them succeed on academic tasks. However, word callers are not as cognitively flexible as their peers. These children tend to have an inflexible focus on single text elements, such as sounds, preventing them from considering texts' meanings and hindering their reading comprehension.

The Research Base

In Chapter 3 you read about research that shows that the ability to think flexibly about sounds and meanings of printed words, assessed with the sound-meaning flexible thinking assessment, contributes to reading comprehension in beginning readers (Cartwright et al. 2010), second to fourth graders (Cartwright 2002, 2006), and adults (Cartwright 2007). As you might expect, sound-meaning flexibility improves with age (Cartwright, Isaac, and Dandy 2006), although it varies considerably at each grade level (see Figure 3–7), with some children performing better than some adults.

Because other researchers had found that cognitive flexibility could be taught (e.g., Bigler and Liben 1992), I wondered whether we might be able to teach sound-meaning flexible thinking, too, and whether improvements in sound-meaning flexibility might also improve reading comprehension. So, I tested second- to fourth-grade children on sound-meaning flexible thinking, decoding, verbal ability, and reading comprehension, using the Woodcock Reading Mastery Tests—Revised (WRMT) Passage Comprehension subtest, Form G (Woodcock 1987), which requires students to fill in missing words from prose passages (Cartwright 2002, 2006). Then, I randomly assigned students to three groups: a group that received sound-meaning flexible thinking lessons, a group that received general, color-shape flexible thinking lessons (they sorted pictures by color and shape at the same time), and a control group with whom I played dominoes so that those students spent an equal amount of time with me. The groups did not differ significantly on WRMT Passage Comprehension scores, decoding skill, sound-meaning flexible thinking, or verbal ability before the intervention. Students were taught individually, across five lessons, and those who received one-to-one sound-meaning flexible thinking lessons showed significant improvements in reading comprehension (tested with the WRMT Passage Comprehension subtest, Form H), but the students who received general flexible thinking lessons or played dominoes with me did not (see Figure 4–1). Similar improvements occurred for students' sound-meaning flexible thinking.

These findings were encouraging, but I realized that a one-to-one intervention was not always practical in typical classrooms. I wondered whether teachers could deliver the sound-meaning flexible thinking lessons in a small-group format. When colleagues at a local elementary school told me they were interested in trying the flexible thinking lessons with their students, this provided the perfect opportunity to adapt the intervention for small-group instruction (Cartwright, Clause, and Schmidt 2007). The teachers were reading teachers, and they selected second- to fifth-grade struggling readers who they thought would benefit from the flexible thinking lessons. Students were already assigned to pull-out reading groups for supplemental instruction. Half of those groups were assigned to receive the flexible thinking lessons during their small-group instruction time with a reading teacher, one lesson per week for five weeks. The remaining groups received their regular small-group reading instruction with a reading teacher. Just as I had found with the one-to-one instruction, the students who received small-group sound-meaning flexible thinking lessons showed significant improvements in reading comprehension on two measures: the

FIGURE 4–1

Effects of One-to-One Flexible Thinking Lessons

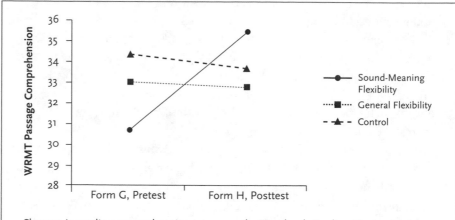

Changes in reading comprehension scores on the Woodcock Reading Mastery Tests (Woodcock 1987) after the individually administered five-lesson sound-meaning flexible thinking intervention (Cartwright 2002)

school's quarterly reading assessment, which required students to read passages and answer questions about them (see Figure 4–2), and the researcher-administered WRMT Passage Comprehension subtest (see Figure 4–3). These findings were particularly important, because they showed that multiple measures of comprehension improved: the school-based assessment required students to answer typical comprehension questions after having read passages, whereas the researcher-administered measure required students to infer appropriate words for missing spots in passages. We saw similar improvements in children's sound-meaning flexible thinking.

FIGURE 4–2

Effects of Small-Group Flexible Thinking Lessons: School Assessments

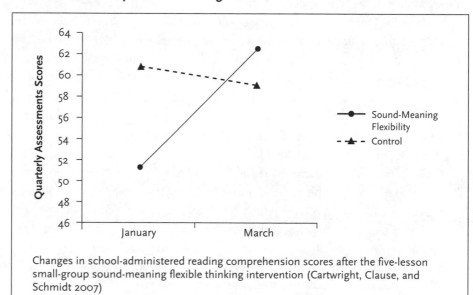

Changes in school-administered reading comprehension scores after the five-lesson small-group sound-meaning flexible thinking intervention (Cartwright, Clause, and Schmidt 2007)

FIGURE 4–3

Effects of Small-Group Flexible Thinking Lessons: Researcher Assessments

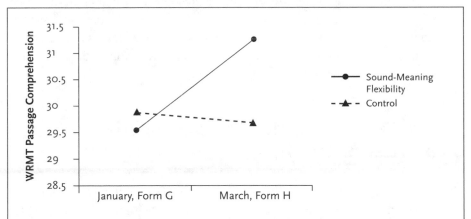

Changes in researcher-administered reading comprehension scores on the Woodcock Reading Mastery Tests (Woodcock 1987) after the five-lesson small-group sound-meaning flexible thinking intervention (Cartwright, Clause, and Schmidt 2007)

Taken together, the research on sound-meaning flexible thinking shows that it is important for reading comprehension at all levels of reading proficiency, from first graders to adults. And, these findings also show that when second- to fifth-grade students are taught to think more flexibly about sounds and meanings of words, whether in one-to-one or small-group instructional contexts, their reading comprehension improves. As I noted in Chapter 3, some teachers have asked how flexible thinking skill transfers to reading comprehension because sorting cards seems so different from reading connected text. In essence, the ability to think flexibly about sounds and meanings facilitates—rather than transfers to—comprehension by providing readers the ability to pay attention to both sounds and meaning while reading, which enables them to broaden their words-only focus to include meaning. In the remainder of this chapter I will describe the sound-meaning flexible thinking lessons so that you can try them with your students. You may be wondering whether these children's comprehension improved for a long time. The students in the small-group study received one lesson per week, across an entire marking period, and their comprehension improved from January to March. The researcher-administered test of comprehension was completed in the weeks following the March school assessment, and the flexible thinking intervention students still showed significant improvements in comprehension, compared to the no-intervention peers. Thus, the gains lasted beyond the marking period in which the series of five lessons occurred. Additional study is needed to determine if the comprehension gains last for a longer time.

The Purpose of the Lessons: Practice with Sounds and Meaning

The sound-meaning flexible thinking intervention is designed to do two things for students, which are accomplished in two steps. First, the intervention makes students aware that there are multiple dimensions to print by having them attend to each dimension independently, meanings and then sounds (or sounds and then meanings), in the same set of words. Next, the intervention gives students practice in thinking flexibly about both dimensions at once until they can do so reliably. This process is repeated with five different sets of words, across five lessons that occur on different days, resulting in improvements in flexible thinking and enabling struggling readers to focus on meaning in addition to sound for improved comprehension.

One-to-One Intervention Lesson: Materials, Steps, Assessment Tips

In this section I will describe the sound-meaning flexible thinking lesson for individual students. In my original intervention study (Cartwright 2002, 2006), children's flexible thinking was assessed with five word sets—one set to teach the task and four sets to assess the students—prior to beginning the intervention (see Chapter 3 for the assessment). In the intervention, students received five individual lessons on different days, with a different word set each time. The five word sets used for the intervention lessons were those that had been used for the assessment, so students had already worked with the word sets prior to the intervention lessons. I recommend assessing your students' flexible thinking before you begin lessons, because that will provide your students important background knowledge necessary to understand the lessons. If you choose not to assess your students before beginning the lessons, you may need to model correct responses for your students, and provide explanations for those responses, before asking your students to try each of the lesson components.

The lesson format for one day's lesson is described below and includes explanation, picture work (as a scaffold), and word work. Especially with struggling readers, pictures are an important scaffold to build understanding and confidence before you introduce the words. After the first two or three lessons, if your student seems to grasp the word tasks, you may not need to continue to use the pictures.

Materials

- a desk or table in a quiet area where you can work one-to-one with your student
- 2 × 2 matrix
- one set of picture cards (to scaffold understanding)
- one set of word cards
- an Individual Lesson Record Sheet (see Figure 4–4 for the reproducible sheet)
- a clipboard (to hold the record sheet in your lap, out of the student's view)
- a pencil or pen to record your student's progress

FIGURE 4–4

Individual Sound-Meaning Flexibility Intervention Record Sheet

(Use one record sheet for each student for the entire five-lesson intervention; each lesson occurs on a different day.)

STUDENT NAME: _____ TEACHER: _____ GRADE: _____

NOTE DATE & CARD SETS USED	PICTURE SINGLE SORTS	PICTURE COMPLETION	WORD SINGLE SORTS	WORD COMPLETION 1	WORD COMPLETION 2	WORD COMPLETION 3	WORD COMPLETION 4
LESSON 1 Date: Pictures:							
Words:	Notes:						
LESSON 2 Date: Pictures:							
Words:	Notes:						
LESSON 3 Date: Pictures:							
Words:	Notes:						
LESSON 4 Date: Pictures:							
Words:	Notes:						
LESSON 5 Date: Pictures:							
Words:	Notes:						

Explain the Task

Explanation takes 1–2 minutes, depending on grade level and your student's grasp of the concept of flexible thinking.

Explain the purpose of the lesson to your student, saying something like, "Today we are going to do something fun with cards that will also help you with your reading. Good readers think about lots of things when they read, like letters, sounds, words, and what words mean. That's called being flexible, because your brain can think of lots of things at the same time. This lesson will help you do that!" Use whatever explanation works for your student. (One reading teacher with whom I have worked told her students that being flexible meant that their brains were "bendy," drawing on children's understanding of physical flexibility.)

You may want to show your student Figure 4–5, which depicts the flexible and inflexible thinkers from Chapter 2, but this time they are thinking about features of print. Explain the picture to your student by pointing to the reader on the right and saying something like, "See, this reader is just thinking about letters and sounds when she reads." Then point to the reader on the left and say, "But, this reader is thinking about letters and sounds, the word, and what the word means!" Again, offer whatever explanation is necessary to ensure that your student understands the concept.

FIGURE 4–5

Flexible and Inflexible Readers

Picture Work

Picture work takes approximately 5 minutes.

As I noted earlier, with struggling readers it is often useful to start with pictures that can be sorted by color and type. All children, regardless of reading ability, have experience with categorizing objects by color and type. Additionally, I have found that children who sort pictures before they sort words have a better understanding of the sound-meaning word sorts (Cartwright 1997). As I noted before, once your student understands the nature of the intervention tasks you no longer need to use the picture scaffold for the intervention lessons.

Single Sorts with Pictures: Noticing Two Dimensions

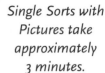

Single Sorts with Pictures take approximately 3 minutes.

This portion of the lesson does not involve the 2 × 2 matrix, so keep it hidden for now. The purpose of the single sorts is simply to make your student aware that there are two features (or dimensions) by which the cards can be sorted by asking the student to do two independent sorts. You should vary the order of the sorts (color first or type first) across lessons.

- Tell your student, "I have some picture cards that can be sorted two ways: by color and by what kind of thing is on the card."
- Then, give your student a set of twelve pictures, and say, "Sort these cards into two piles by what *color* they are." (Emphasize the word *color* in your directions.) Your student should make two piles with six cards in each pile, sorted by color (see Figure 4–6). Students rarely make mistakes on this portion of the lesson. If your student does make an error, however, such as misplacing a card, just rearrange the sort and offer an explanation (e.g., "I'm going to put the banana over here because it's yellow, just like these others").

FIGURE 4–6

Picture Single Sort by Color

A correct sort by color on the Picture Single Sort portion of the lesson: All six red cards are in one pile, and all six yellow cards are in another pile.

- Next, collect the cards and reshuffle them. Tell your student, "Now I want you to sort these cards into two piles by *what kind of thing* is on the card." (As before, emphasize the sorting dimension in your directions.) Your student should sort the cards into two piles of six cards each by type, such as fruits and flowers, regardless of color (see Figure 4–7). Typically, the second sort is a little more difficult than the first, because children must switch sorting rules, which requires a bit of cognitive flexibility. (This type of switching develops with age; see e.g., Zelazo et al. 2003.) As before, you should correct any mistakes and explain why.

FIGURE 4–7

Picture Single Sort by Type

A correct sort by type on the Picture Single Sort portion of the lesson: All six fruits are in one pile, and all six flowers are in another pile.

- Once your student completes both individual sorts, you should place a check mark in the appropriate box on the Individual Lesson Record to indicate that Picture Single Sorts are complete (see Figure 4–8).
- Collect the cards from your student and reshuffle them.

FIGURE 4–8

Record Picture Single Sorts

NOTE DATE & CARD SETS USED	PICTURE SINGLE SORTS	PICTURE COMPLETION	WORD SINGLE SORTS	WORD COMPLETION 1	WORD COMPLETION 2	WORD COMPLETION 3	WORD COMPLETION 4
LESSON 1 **Date:** 6/2 **Pictures:** Fruit and Flowers **Words:** /b/ and /t/ Vehicles and Animals	✓						
	Notes:						

Record the student's Picture Single Sort on the Individual Lesson Record Sheet.

Matrix Completion with Pictures: Practicing Flexible Thinking

- Place the 2 × 2 matrix on the table. If your student has completed the flexible thinking assessment (see Chapter 3), then he or she might say something like, "I know how to do this!" Explain to your student that you are going to do something new with the cards today.

- Place three cards in the matrix, sorted by color and type, with an open spot in the matrix (see Figure 4–9). Ideally, you should vary the location of the open spot in the matrix across lessons to foster optimal flexibility.

Matrix Completion with Pictures takes approximately 2 minutes.

FIGURE 4–9

Format for Picture Matrix Completion

You should vary the position of the empty spot across lessons.

- Hand your student the remaining nine cards in the set, point to the empty spot in the matrix, and say, "Find a card that goes here." The student should look through the remaining cards and choose a card that completes a 2 × 2 sort, placing it in the open spot in the matrix. For the sort in Figure 4–8, any of the three red flowers in the stack would complete the sort appropriately.

- If your student chooses correctly, offer positive feedback and ask the student why that card works. For example, you might say, "Good job! Can you tell me why that one goes there?" The student should explain the choice in terms of the two sorting dimensions: color and type.

- If your student chooses incorrectly, guide him to the appropriate response. For example, if your student chooses a red fruit for the open spot in Figure 4–8, then you might point to the rows of the matrix and say, "These are yellow and these are red, so that works." Then point to the columns and say, "These are fruits, so these need to be . . ." Pause to see if your student can complete the sentence, indicating the realization that a red flower must fill the missing spot.

- You may repeat the matrix completion process if you feel it is necessary to ensure that your student understands it. Once your student completes a matrix successfully, mark the appropriate spot on the Individual Lesson Record Sheet (see Figure 4–10). If your student had difficulty, you may also wish to note the fact in the appropriate location on the record sheet.

- Remove the picture cards and the 2 × 2 matrix from the table.

FIGURE 4–10

Record Picture Completion

NOTE DATE & CARD SETS USED	PICTURE SINGLE SORTS	PICTURE COMPLETION	WORD SINGLE SORTS	WORD COMPLETION 1	WORD COMPLETION 2	WORD COMPLETION 3	WORD COMPLETION 4
LESSON 1 **Date:** 6/2 **Pictures:** Fruit and Flowers **Words:** /b/ and /t/ Vehicles and Animals	✓	✓					
	Notes:						

Record the student's Picture Completion on the Individual Lesson Record Sheet. You may wish to note if the student does not get it on the first try.

Word Work

The work with word cards is the critical part of the lesson that helps the student learn to think flexibly about multiple features of print: sounds and meanings. The work with word cards is identical to the work with the picture cards, *except that the child must provide four consecutive correct responses on the matrix completion portion of the lesson.* It is important to note that your explanations of this task (for your students) should refer to *sounds* and not letters, as the purpose of the task is to get children thinking about sounds and meanings. Introduce the new task to your student by saying something like, "Now we're going to do the same things with word cards."

Single Sorts with Words: Noticing Two Dimensions

Single Sorts with Words take approximately 3 minutes.

As before, this portion of the lesson does not involve the 2 × 2 matrix, so keep it hidden from view. Recall that the purpose of the single sorts is simply to make your student aware that there are two features (or dimensions) by which the cards can be sorted by asking the student to do two independent sorts. You should vary the order of the sorts (sound first or meaning first) across lessons.

- Tell your student, "These word cards can be sorted two ways: by how they sound and by what they mean."

- Then, give your student a set of twelve words, and say, "Sort these cards into two piles by *how they sound*." (Emphasize the sorting dimension in your directions.) Your student should make two piles with six cards in each pile, sorted by initial sound (see Figure 4–11). Students rarely make mistakes on this portion of the lesson. If your student does make an error, however, such as misplacing a card, just rearrange the sort and offer an explanation (e.g., "I'm going to put *bus* over here because it's a /b/ word, just like these others").

FIGURE 4–11

Word Single Sort by Sound

A correct sort by sound on the Word Single Sort portion of the lesson: All six /b/ words are in one pile, and all six /t/ words are in another pile.

- Next, collect the cards and reshuffle them. Tell your student, "Now I want you to sort these cards into two piles by *what they mean*." (As before, emphasize the sorting dimension in your directions.) Your student should sort the cards into two piles of six cards each by meaning, such as vehicles and animals, regardless of sound (see Figure 4–12). As I noted previously, the second sort is typically a little more difficult than the first, because children must switch sorting rules. As before, you should correct any mistakes and explain why.

FIGURE 4–12

Word Single Sort by Meaning

A correct sort by meaning on the Word Single Sort portion of the lesson: All six vehicle words are in one pile, and all six animal words are in another pile.

- Once your student completes both individual sorts, you should place a check mark in the appropriate box on the Individual Lesson Record to indicate that the Word Single Sorts are complete (see Figure 4–13).
- Collect the cards from your student and reshuffle them.

FIGURE 4–13

Record Word Single Sorts

NOTE DATE & CARD SETS USED	PICTURE SINGLE SORTS	PICTURE COMPLETION	WORD SINGLE SORTS	WORD COMPLETION 1	WORD COMPLETION 2	WORD COMPLETION 3	WORD COMPLETION 4
LESSON 1 **Date:** 6/2 **Pictures:** Fruit and Flowers **Words:** /b/ and /t/ Vehicles and Animals	✓	✓	✓				
	Notes:						

Record the student's Word Single Sorts on the Individual Lesson Record Sheet. You may wish to note if the student does not get it on the first try.

Matrix Completion with Words: Practicing Flexible Thinking

- Return the 2 × 2 matrix to the table.

- Place three word cards in the matrix sorted by sound and meaning, with an open spot in the matrix (see Figure 4–14). Ideally, you should vary the location of the open spot in the matrix across lessons to foster optimal flexibility.

FIGURE 4–14

Format for Word Matrix Completion

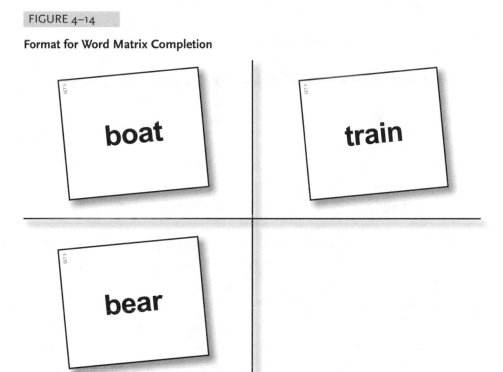

You should vary the position of the empty spot across lessons.

- Hand your student the remaining nine cards in the set, point to the empty spot in the matrix, and say, "Find a card that goes here." The student should look through the remaining cards and choose a card that completes a 2 × 2 sort, placing it in the open spot in the matrix. For the sort in Figure 4–14, any of the three animals that start with /t/ will complete the sort appropriately (e.g., *tiger*, *toad*, or *turkey*).

- If your student chooses correctly, offer positive feedback and ask the student why that card works. For example, you might say, "Good job! Can you tell me why that one goes there?" The student should explain the choice in terms of the two sorting dimensions: sound and meaning.

- Place a check mark in the appropriate box on the Individual Lesson Record Sheet to indicate your student's progress.

- If your student chooses incorrectly, guide her to the appropriate response. For example, if your student chooses another vehicle that starts with /t/, such as *tractor*, then you might point to the columns of the matrix and say, "These are /b/ words and these are /t/ words, so that works." Then point to the rows and

Matrix Completion with Words takes approximately 5–10 minutes because it requires that your student get four consecutive completions correct; some students may get all four on the first try, whereas other students may need additional attempts to reach the goal.

say, "These are vehicles (or transportation, or things that go, whatever works for your student), so these need to be . . ." Pause to see if your student can complete the sentence, indicating the realization that the missing word must be an animal that starts with /t/.

This is the point where Matrix Completion with Words differs from the Picture portion. You must repeat the Word Completion portion of the lesson until your student is able to get four consecutive correct responses. That is, your student must be able to get four in a row correct before the lesson is complete. If your student provides an incorrect response before reaching four in a row correct, then you must begin counting responses again from one. Note that the criterion of four consecutive responses is critically important to ensure that your student can reliably consider the sounds and meanings of words flexibly. As you repeat the matrix completions, you should proceed as follows.

- After your student finishes a matrix completion, take up the cards, reshuffle them, and place three new cards in the matrix, sorted by sound and meaning. Vary the open spot in the matrix to foster greater flexibility on the task. Give your student the remaining cards, and have him or her choose an appropriate card to complete the 2 × 2 sort.

- As before, note correct responses on the Lesson Record Sheet, and guide your student to appropriate responses if he or she responds incorrectly.

- Repeat the Word Matrix Completion process until your student provides four consecutive correct responses.

- Mark correct responses on the Individual Lesson Record form. If, for example, a child provides two correct responses and then misses the third, you must start over and begin counting responses again from one. In this case, cross out the check marks you made on the Lesson Record form and begin a new row of check marks (see Figure 4–15).

Issues of Timing

The complete intervention includes five lessons like the one I just described, with each of the five lessons occurring on different instructional days with different word and picture sets. As you can see from the time estimates, the individual intervention takes 15–20 minutes, depending on how long it takes your student to finish the four consecutive Word Completions. Additionally, once your student understands the lesson, you do not need to use picture work, which reduces the instructional time by five minutes.

Recording Your Student's Performance

Figure 4–15 shows Brittany's performance on her first lesson. She missed the first Picture Completion, which is noted in the "Notes" section on the Lesson Record. On the Word Completions, she got two correct and then missed one. Then, she got three correct and missed one. Finally, she got four in a row correct. Each time she missed a Word Completion I crossed out the check marks and started counting again from one. Noting students' responses this way provides important

FIGURE 4–15

Record Word Completions

NOTE DATE & CARD SETS USED	PICTURE SINGLE SORTS	PICTURE COMPLETION	WORD SINGLE SORTS	WORD COMPLETION 1	WORD COMPLETION 2	WORD COMPLETION 3	WORD COMPLETION 4
LESSON 1 Date: 6/2 Pictures: Fruit and Flowers Words: /b/ and /t/ Vehicles and Animals	✓	✓	✓	~~✓~~ ~~✓~~ ✓	~~✓~~ ~~✓~~ ✓	~~✓~~ ✓	✓
	Notes: Brittany missed the first picture completion but completed it correctly on the second try. It took her a while to get the reading completions. She initially got two correct and then missed one. Then, she got three correct and missed one. Finally, she got four in a row correct.						

Record the student's Word Completions on the Individual Lesson Record Sheet. Cross out responses when the student misses one, and start counting again. Repeat this procedure until the student gets four in a row correct.

information about the length of time it takes each student to have a solid grasp of the sound-meaning sorts, and the ability to complete four consecutive correct completions indicates a more stable sound-meaning flexibility.

Small-Group Intervention Lesson: Materials, Steps, Assessment Tips

Small-group lessons proceed in much the same way as individual lessons, with explanation, picture work, and word work. These typically occur at a small table where you can face the students with whom you are working. (A horseshoe-shaped table works well for this purpose.) My work with teachers who have implemented the sound-meaning flexible thinking lessons in small groups indicates that the optimal group size is five or fewer students. Keep in mind that when you do the Single Sorts in each lesson, *each student* in the group gets a card set. Similarly, when you do the Matrix Completion portions of the lesson, each student gets a card set and a 2 × 2 matrix. Including more than five students in small groups often results in a chaotic experience for all involved. (Imagine six or more students at a small table, each with a set of twelve cards and a 2 × 2 matrix, and you will understand why it is best to limit the group size to five or fewer students!) One set of materials (picture cards, word cards, and a 2 × 2 matrix) accompanies this book. If you are interested in using the sound-meaning flexible thinking lessons in a small-group format, packages of five sets of materials to support small-group instruction are available as a supplement to this book.

Materials

- six 2 × 2 matrices (enough for you and each student)
- six sets of picture cards (enough for you and each student)
- six sets of word cards (enough for you and each student)
- markers for the empty spots in the Matrix Completion portions of the lesson (plastic chips, pennies, or paper clips work well for this purpose)
- a clipboard (to hold the record sheet in your lap, out of the students' view)
- a pencil or pen to record your students' progress
- Small-Group Lesson Record Sheets, one for each lesson (see Figure 4–16 for the reproducible sheet)

What Changes for Small-Group Instruction?

The lesson format for small groups is almost identical to that for the one-to-one lessons: you will explain the task, engage your students in Single Sorts and Matrix Completion with Pictures, engage your students in Single Sorts and Matrix Completion with Words, and you will record students' responses on the Small-Group Lesson Record Sheet in the same way that you did for individual lessons. (Note that you need one Small-Group Record Sheet for each of the five intervention lessons.) Because you will do individual Matrix Completions for each student in your group (for both Pictures and Words), those portions of the lesson take a bit longer than for the individual lessons, expanding your total lesson time by approximately 10–15 minutes. Once children understand the lesson activities, you no longer need to use pictures, which reduces the lesson by at least five minutes. Refer to the directions for the individual intervention to complete the small-group lesson. Slight modifications to the lesson format are necessary to accommodate small-group instruction, and these are described in the following sections.

Explanation

The explanation portion of the small-group lesson can proceed as a group discussion. Explain flexibility in ways that your students will understand. Build on the students' existing knowledge of the concept, and ensure they understand that the lessons will help them think more flexibly, like good readers.

Picture Work

When you begin the picture work, you should explain the task just as you would for the individual lesson. Give each child a set of picture cards (all children should have the same cards), and proceed through the single sorts as you would for the individual lesson. Make sure you are able to examine each student's sort before the cards are reshuffled for the second independent sort along the other dimension (color or shape). Record your students' Picture Single Sorts on the Small-Group Lesson Record Sheet, just as you would for the individual lesson. Reshuffle each student's cards and set them aside.

FIGURE 4–16

Small-Group Sound-Meaning Flexible Thinking Lesson Record Sheet

(Use one record sheet for each small-group lesson; you will need five record sheets for the entire five-lesson intervention.)

Intervention Session (circle one): 1 2 3 4 5

PICTURE CARDS: _____ WORD CARDS: _____

TEACHER: _____ GRADE: _____ DATE: _____

STUDENT NAME	PICTURE SINGLE SORTS	PICTURE COMPLETION	WORD SINGLE SORTS	WORD COMPLETION 1	WORD COMPLETION 2	WORD COMPLETION 3	WORD COMPLETION 4
1.							
Notes:							
2.							
Notes:							
3.							
Notes:							
4.							
Notes:							
5.							
Notes:							

For Picture Completions, explain the task as you would for the individual intervention and then model the procedure for the students with your set of materials. Place three cards in the matrix, sorted by color and type (see Figure 4–9 for an example), and have the students in the group work together to produce a correct response. Be sure to explain why a particular picture is appropriate for the open space. After the initial modeling of the Matrix Completion, the small-group lesson proceeds like the individual lesson. You will work individually with each student, one student at a time. For example, if you are at a horseshoe table, you might work with the leftmost child first, and proceed around the table, working with one student at a time. Give each student a 2 × 2 matrix, and use each student's set of cards to select three cards for his or her matrix. After you place three cards in a student's matrix, give the child the remaining nine cards, point to the empty spot, and tell the student to "Find a card that goes here." Before you move on to the next student, be sure to mark the corner of the empty spot in the matrix with an object (e.g., a plastic chip, penny, or paper clip) so that you will remember which spot was empty when you return to that student's work (see Figure 4–17). Once you place three cards in each student's matrix and the students are working on finding cards to fill the empty spots, you should return to the first child's work and assess the student's accuracy. For each student, follow the directions for accurate and inaccurate responses provided in the description of the individual lesson, above. When all five students have successfully managed a picture completion, you should move on to word work. Remember, once your students understand the nature of the intervention tasks, picture work is not necessary.

FIGURE 4–17

Mark the Open Spot

Mark the empty spot for Small-Group Matrix Completions with a plastic chip or another object so that you remember which spot to check when you return to a student's work.

Word Work

Introduce the word work in the same way that you would for individual lessons. Then, give each child a set of words, and complete the single sorts as described in the individual intervention directions. Be sure to examine each student's sorts for accuracy, and mark the appropriate space on the Lesson Record Sheet once each student achieves a correct response. Reshuffle each student's cards and set them aside before moving on to Matrix Completions.

Before providing materials to each student, model a Word Completion for the group. Place three cards in your matrix, sorted by sound and meaning, and allow group members to work together to determine which word(s) fit in the open spot in the matrix (see Figure 4–14). Then, give each student a 2 × 2 matrix, and proceed with the Word Completions, one student at a time, just as you did for the small-group Picture Completions.

Recall that in the Picture Completion you marked the open spot in each child's matrix so that you knew which spot to check when you returned to the student's work. Those markers provide the opportunity to turn the Word Completions into a game for the students. Just as in the individual lessons, each student must complete four Word Completions correctly before returning to class. Tell your students, "Each time you find a correct word to fill the empty spot, you get to keep a chip (or clip, or penny), and when you earn four chips in a row, you win the game! But, if you miss one, I get to take all the chips, and you have to start over." Students really enjoy the chip-collecting component of small-group Word Completions. And, the chips help you keep track of the number of correct consecutive responses provided by each student as well as the locations of the empty spots in students' matrices. Continue around the table, working with one student at a time, until each student achieves four consecutive correct Word Completions. Refer to the individual lesson directions for instructions on how to record students' responses on the Lesson Record Sheet.

Closing Notes

A shorthand version of the lesson description—an Intervention Lesson Guide—is provided in Figure 4–18 for your convenience, and the Picture Scaffold to support your explanations to students is provided in Figure 4–19. I offer the following final thoughts about the interventions to aid your plans for implementing them in your classroom. Whereas the individual lesson format provides you the opportunity to work closely with single students who may need intensive, one-to-one support, the small-group lesson format provides students opportunities to learn from one another as they participate in the lesson. For example, students see one another choose words for Word Completions, and they also benefit by hearing the feedback that you provide their peers. You may find, however, that some students are distracted by having others around them in the small-group format. These differences should help you determine which format is best for your students.

FIGURE 4–18

Sound-Meaning Flexibility Thinking Intervention Lesson Guide

Three Intervention Steps for Five Lessons: 1. Explain, 2. Single Sorts, 3. Matrix Completion

EXPLAIN FLEXIBILITY (1 to 2 minutes*)	MATERIALS: • Picture of flexible thinkers	EXPLAIN (1–2 minutes) Use your own words to explain flexibility to your students in a way that they will understand: **"Good readers think about lots of things at one time."**	
PICTURE WORK (scaffold) (5 minutes*) (You can omit picture work once students understand the word activities.)	MATERIALS: **Individual** • set of 12 picture cards for student **Small Group** • set of 12 picture cards for teacher • one set of 12 picture cards for each student	SINGLE SORTS: **Noticing Two Dimensions** (3 minutes) • Have children sort into 2 piles one way (color or type): **"Sort your cards by what color they are."** • Reshuffle cards. • Have children sort into 2 new piles the other way: **"Now sort your cards by what kind they are."** • *Place check marks on Lesson Record Sheet to indicate that each student reclassifies picture cards.*	EXAMPLE all red all yellow and reshuffle, and then... all flowers all fruits and
	MATERIALS: **Individual** • picture cards and 2 x 2 matrix for student **Small Group** • picture cards and 2 x 2 matrix for teacher • picture cards and 2 x 2 matrix for each student	MATRIX COMPLETION: **Practicing Flexible Thinking** (2 minutes) • For small group instruction: Place 2 x 2 matrix on table, place 3 cards in matrix, and **model correct choice for empty spot.** • For individual and small-group instruction, for each student: Place 2 x 2 matrix in front of student; using each student's cards, place 3 cards in student's matrix, sorted by color and type; mark empty spot with chip in small-group instruction; give student remaining cards, and ask student(s) to **"find a card that goes here."** • *Place check marks on Lesson Record Sheet to indicate that each student chooses correctly; collect 2 x 2 matrices.*	EXAMPLE

Time estimates are for individual instruction; small-group instruction adds approximately 10–15 minutes to the lesson.

Sound-Meaning Flexibility Thinking Intervention Lesson Guide

Three Intervention Steps for Five Lessons: 1. Explain, 2. Single Sorts, 3. Matrix Completion

WORD WORK (8 to 13 minutes*)	MATERIALS:	SINGLE SORTS: Noticing Two Dimensions (3 minutes)	EXAMPLE
	Individual • set of 12 word cards for student **Small Group** • set of 12 word cards for teacher • one set of 12 word cards for each student	• Have children sort into 2 piles one way (sound or meaning): **"Sort your cards by how they sound."** • Reshuffle cards. • Have children sort into 2 new piles the other way: **"Now sort your cards by what they mean."** • *Place check marks on Lesson Record Sheet to indicate that each student reclassifies word cards.*	all vehicles all animals boat and bear reshuffle, and then... all /t/ words all /b/ words train and boat
Important: Students must get four CONSECUTIVE completions correct; if they miss one before they reach a total of four, they must start over at one. In small-group instruction, students earn chips for correct completions; if incorrect, you take chips and students begin again.	MATERIALS: **Individual** • word cards and 2 x 2 matrix for student **Small Group** • word cards and 2 x 2 matrix for teacher • word cards and 2 x 2 matrix for each student • 20 plastic chips or other markers to mark "open" spots in matrix	MATRIX COMPLETION: Practicing Flexible Thinking (5–10 minutes) • For small-group instruction, place one 2 x 2 matrix on table, place 3 cards in matrix, and **model correct choice for empty spot.** • For small-group instruction, explain "rules" for "game": **"Now, it's your turn. When you are right, you get a chip. You need to get FOUR chips in a row. If you miss one, I get to keep your chips, and you start over."** • For individual and small-group instruction, for each student: Place 2 x 2 matrix in front of student; using student's cards, place 3 cards in student's matrix sorted by sound and meaning; mark empty spot with chip for small-group instruction; give student remaining cards, and ask student to **"find a card that goes here."** • Continue, reshuffling cards each time, until each student gets FOUR IN A ROW correct. *Place check marks on Lesson Record Sheet to indicate that each student chooses correctly each time. Cross out and start over when child misses one.*	EXAMPLE boat │ ◯ ────────┼──────── train │ bear

Time estimates are for individual instruction; small-group instruction adds approximately 10–15 minutes to the lesson.

FIGURE 4–19

Picture Scaffold for Flexible Thinking Lessons

Keep in mind that for both intervention formats, once you find that the students in your group understand the nature of the intervention activities, the picture work is no longer necessary. This is an important consideration for planning blocks of time for lessons. Your first small-group lesson may take you as long as 30–40 minutes because you and your students are learning a new instructional routine. However, as you and the students become more fluent at the lesson's components, and you omit picture work, you can complete a small-group lesson in about 15–20 minutes. (Some teachers with whom I have worked have decided to split the first lesson into two sessions in order to fit it into their instructional schedule.) Finally, for both lesson formats, it is important to note that because students may reach the criterion of four consecutive correct responses earlier or later than their peers, you will have some students who complete the lesson earlier (or later) than others.

How Does This Help You?

Questions to Consider

- How are the sorting activities in these flexible thinking lessons different from other sorting activities you have used? How might these differences benefit your students?

- Do you have students now whom you think might benefit from the flexible thinking intervention? Why do you think so?

- If you choose to try small-group instruction, the first small-group lesson may take a bit longer than your typical small-group lesson (i.e., 30–40 minutes). How can you adapt your instructional schedule to incorporate this initial, longer lesson?

5

Flexing Thinking with Laughter

Jokes, Riddles, and Other Wordplay Activities

In the last two chapters we focused on children's ability to think about words' sounds and meanings simultaneously, and we learned how to help word callers shift from a sound-only focus to a more meaning-focused approach to print. Sometimes our students need extra help thinking flexibly about words' meanings for optimal comprehension. Because words often have multiple meanings, the ability to call up the *right* meaning for a particular context affects understanding. (Consider, for example, the word *jam*, which can appear next to *traffic* or next to *strawberry*, resulting in very different interpretations of *jam*'s meaning.) In other instances authors (and speakers) use multiple meanings to convey humorous messages, which will be missed if students can't consider the multiple meanings in texts.

Remember this?

> What's black and white and red all over?
>
> A newspaper!

Or this:

> A duck goes to the pharmacy counter to buy some lip balm.
>
> "How would you like to pay for this?" asks the pharmacist.
>
> "Oh, just put it on my bill," the duck replied.

Or this:

> What did the dinosaur say when he ate a clown?
>
> "That tasted funny!"

Chances are, if you work with elementary school children, you have heard classics like these over and over. As much as we may groan at their cornball humor, on some level we are glad they keep bubbling up generation after generation. And it turns out, the endurance of riddles is no accident, as they perform a valuable function in children's development—perhaps especially for those children who need to become more flexible in their thinking about print. Here's how.

Jokes and riddles often include ambiguous words, such as homonyms and homophones, to achieve their humorous result (see Figure 5–1 for more examples of riddles that rely on verbal ambiguity). Remember, homonyms are words with the same spelling and pronunciation but with different meanings. The word *bill* in the duck joke, for example, is a homonym. Homophones, on the other hand, are words with the same pronunciation but different spellings and meanings, such as *red* and *read* in the famous riddle about the newspaper.

FIGURE 5–1

Examples of Riddles That Rely on Verbal Ambiguity

Q: Why was the baby ant confused?
A: Because all of his uncles were aunts

Q: How much is a skunk worth?
A: One scent

Q: What building has the most stories?
A: The library

Q: Why wasn't the moon so smart?
A: Because the sun is brighter

Q: What nails do carpenters hate to hit?
A: Fingernails

Q: Why is six afraid of seven?
A: Because seven eight nine.

Q: What did the dinosaur say when he ate a clown?
A: That tasted funny.

Q: What did one ocean say to the other?
A: Nothing, they just waved.

(These riddles were gathered from http://kids.niehs.nih.gov/jokes.htm#jokes, http://tiki.oneworld.net/fun/jokes/jokes.html, www.azkidsnet.com/riddles.htm, and www.squiglysplayhouse.com/JokesAndRiddles/index.html on February 23, 2009.)

The misperceptions that arise from the dual meanings of homonyms and homophones are what we find humorous. Even in everyday conversation, children sometimes misperceive ambiguous words' meanings. I remember one afternoon when I picked my daughter up at school and she said, "Mom, Ms. Mary was fired today. I bet that hurt!" Clearly, Jessie had interpreted *fired* to mean something to do with an actual flame rather than termination of Mary's employment. In this instance, Jessie did not know the alternate meaning of the homonym, *fire*. This example illustrates an important point about children's understanding of ambiguous words: to grasp the verbal ambiguity that often results from homonyms and homophones, children must have knowledge of the two, often incompatible, meanings of these words. However, even if children know both meanings, to understand the humor in jokes and riddles that rely on verbal ambiguity, children also must be able to consider simultaneously both of the meanings associated with ambiguous words. That is, they must hold two ideas in mind at once.

INSIGHT FROM CHILDREN'S THINKING

As we learned in Chapter 2, students who lack cognitive flexibility have difficulty thinking about two ideas at once, especially when the ideas are very different from one another, as is often the case with homonyms' and homophones' multiple meanings. Word callers' tendency to think about one idea at a time means that they are less likely than skilled comprehenders to note multiple meanings for words or to understand riddles that rely on verbal ambiguity (Yuill and Oakhill 1991; Yuill 1996). Thus, when word callers encounter ambiguous words in text and make inappropriate initial interpretations of those words, they are less likely than their peers with better comprehension to notice alternative meanings that would better fit the text's context and preserve comprehension (van der Schoot et al. 2009).

The Research Base

In fact, lack of awareness of multiple possible meanings of words is related to poor comprehension in children, adolescents, and adults (Gernsbacher and Robertson 1995; Yuill 1996, 2007; Zipke 2007). However, children's comprehension improves when we teach them how to recognize and consider multiple meanings of ambiguous words and sentences (Yuill 1996, 2007; Zipke 2008; Zipke, Ehri, and Cairns 2009).

Working with school children in Brighton, a town on the southern coast of England, Nicola Yuill (1996, 2007; also see Yuill et al. 2008 for a review) was one of the first researchers to explore the use of ambiguous words to improve word callers' awareness of texts' multiple meanings. She knew that metalinguistic awareness—children's ability to reflect on language—was related to reading comprehension (see Nagy 2007 for more on metalinguistic awareness); and she reasoned that because children typically have much experience with jokes and riddles, these language forms might provide a useful way to help children become more aware of words' multiple meanings, with positive effects on reading comprehension. So, she engaged children who fit the word caller profile in several activities, such as

- defining and generating words with multiple meanings
- explaining multiple meanings in ambiguous sentences (e.g., *The keys were found by the dog.* This sentence could mean that the keys were next to the dog, or it could mean that the dog found the keys.)
- explaining ambiguity in compound words (e.g., *butterfly* refers to a type of insect, but it could also refer to a winged food item)
- explaining jokes and riddles that rely on verbal ambiguity (e.g., the riddles with which I opened the chapter).

Yuill (1996) found that seven- to eight-year-old word callers who experienced these activities in 30-minute sessions, once per week, for seven weeks showed improved comprehension, such that their comprehension scores were similar to that of good comprehenders in the study. In a second, similar study, Yuill (2007) had pairs of children discuss homonyms and homophones, ambiguous sentences, and riddles base on verbal ambiguity, which were presented on a computer. As was found in the initial study, these activities also improved children's reading comprehension.

While Nicola Yuill's research was conducted with elementary children in the U.K., Marcy Zipke and her colleagues have extended this work to U.S. elementary school children (Zipke 2008; Zipke, Ehri, and Cairns 2009). Zipke's intervention involved activities that were similar to those used by Nicola Yuill (1996, 2007), except that Zipke added an additional activity, which involved teaching children to identify ambiguous words in popular children's books that provide opportunities to discuss multiple meanings. Perhaps most well known for its play with word meanings, the Amelia Bedelia children's book series, by Peggy Parish and Herman Parish, centers around the humorous exploits of Amelia Bedelia, a maid who makes numerous mistakes because she misinterprets common word usages. For example, in the first book in the series, when Amelia Bedelia was asked by her employers to "draw the drapes," she drew a picture of the drapes rather than opening them, much to her employers' surprise (Parish 1963). Mistakes such as this one offer the opportunity to discuss multiple meanings for homonyms like *draw*, and Zipke (2008; Zipke, Ehri, and Cairns 2009) used these texts in her intervention. (See Figure 5–2 for a list of books that promote discussion of multiple meanings, including Amelia Bedelia books and other books that use wordplay.) Children were taught to identify multiple meanings in homonyms and homophones, ambiguous sentences, riddles, and texts, resulting in significant improvement in children's reading comprehension.

FIGURE 5–2

Books That Support Discussion of Multiple Text Meanings

Barretta, Gene. 2007. *Dear Deer.* New York: Henry Holt.	Parish, Herman. 1995. *Good Driving, Amelia Bedelia.* New York: HarperCollins.
Cleary, Brian. 2007. *How Much Can a Bare Bear Bear? What Are Homonyms and Homophones?* Minneapolis: First Avenue Editions.	Parish, Herman. 1997. *Bravo, Amelia Bedelia.* New York: HarperCollins.
Fox, Mem. 1984. *Wilfrid Gordon McDonald Partridge.* La Jolla, CA: Kane/Miller.	Parish, Herman. 1999. *Amelia Bedelia 4 Mayor.* New York: HarperCollins.
Frasier, Debra. 2000. *Miss Alaineus: A Vocabulary Disaster.* New York: Houghton Mifflin Harcourt.	Parish, Herman. 2002. *Calling Doctor Amelia Bedelia.* New York: HarperCollins.
Gwynne, Fred. 1970. *The King Who Rained (Stories to Go!).* New York: Aladdin.	Parish, Herman. 2003. *Amelia Bedelia, Bookworm.* New York: HarperCollins.
Gwynne, Fred. 1976. *A Chocolate Moose for Dinner (Stories to Go!).* New York: Aladdin.	Parish, Herman. 2003. *Amelia Bedelia and the Christmas List.* New York: HarperCollins.
Gwynne, Fred. 1988. *A Little Pigeon Toad.* New York: Aladdin.	Parish, Herman. 2004. *Happy Haunting, Amelia Bedelia.* New York: HarperCollins.
Parish, Peggy. 1963. *Amelia Bedelia.* New York: HarperCollins.	Parish, Herman. 2004. *Amelia Bedelia Goes Back to School.* New York: HarperCollins.
Parish, Peggy. 1964. *Thank You, Amelia Bedelia.* New York: HarperCollins.	Parish, Herman. 2005. *Amelia Bedelia, Rocket Scientist?* New York: HarperCollins.
Parish, Peggy. 1966. *Amelia Bedelia and the Surprise Shower.* New York: HarperCollins.	Parish, Herman. 2005. *Be My Valentine, Amelia Bedelia.* New York: HarperCollins.
Parish, Peggy. 1971. *Come Back, Amelia Bedelia.* New York: HarperCollins.	Parish, Herman. 2006. *Amelia Bedelia Under Construction.* New York: HarperCollins.
Parish, Peggy. 1972. *Play Ball, Amelia Bedelia.* New York: HarperCollins.	Parish, Herman. 2007. *Amelia Bedelia's Masterpiece.* New York: HarperCollins.
Parish, Peggy. 1976. *Good Work, Amelia Bedelia.* New York: HarperCollins.	Parish, Herman. 2008. *Amelia Bedelia and the Cat.* New York: HarperCollins.
Parish, Peggy. 1977. *Teach Us, Amelia Bedelia.* New York: HarperCollins.	Parish, Herman. 2008. *Amelia Bedelia Talks Turkey.* New York: HarperCollins.
Parish, Peggy. 1979. *Amelia Bedelia Helps Out.* New York: HarperCollins.	Parish, Herman. 2009. *Amelia Bedelia's First Day of School.* New York: HarperCollins.
Parish, Peggy. 1981. *Amelia Bedelia and the Baby.* New York: HarperCollins.	Park, Barbara. 1993. *Junie B. Jones and a Little Monkey Business.* New York: Random House.
Parish, Peggy. 1985. *Amelia Bedelia Goes Camping.* New York: HarperCollins.	Terban, Marvin. 2007. *Eight Ate: A Feast of Homonym Riddles.* New York: Houghton Mifflin.
Parish, Peggy. 1986. *Merry Christmas, Amelia Bedelia.* New York: HarperCollins.	Truss, Lynn. 2006. *Eats, Shoots & Leaves: Why Commas Really Do Make a Difference!* New York: GP Putnam's Sons.
Parish, Peggy. 1988. *Amelia Bedelia's Family Album.* New York: HarperCollins.	Walton, Rick. 1998. *Why the Banana Split.* Layton, UT: Gibbs Smith.

Close Cousins: Colloquialisms

beat around the bush	hold your horses	raining cats and dogs
draw the drapes	keep your chin up	strip the bed
dress the turkey	lend me your ear	tie the knot
drive me up a wall	let the cat out of the bag	toe the line
flea market	on pins and needles	under the weather
hit the hay	out on a limb	
hit the sack	put a sock in it	

Finally, I would be remiss if I did not note a related activity that has been shown to help upper elementary students who struggle with comprehension, which requires that students pay attention to multiple components of individual words. Several researchers have shown that upper elementary and middle school students' sensitivity to meaningful word parts—or morphemes—such as prefixes, roots, and suffixes, contributes to their reading comprehension (Carlisle 2000; McCutchen, Logan, and Biangardi-Orpe 2009; Nagy, Berninger, and Abbott 2006). Not only that, but when struggling comprehenders are taught to attend to word parts as clues to meaning, their comprehension improves (Katz and Carlisle 2009; Tomesen and Aarnoutse 1998).

The Purpose of the Instructional Activities: Opening Minds to Multiple Meanings

Words and sentences frequently have multiple possible meanings, and readers' ability to consider those meanings affects comprehension. Ambiguous language forms like homonyms, homophones, sentences, compound words, jokes, and riddles—and even sentences with misplaced punctuation (such as those featured in the children's book, *Eats, Shoots & Leaves: Why, Commas Really Do Make a Difference!* by Lynn Truss, see Figure 5–2)—offer opportunities for word callers to practice thinking about multiple meanings at one time, fostering a more flexible approach to text. The instructional activities described in the next section are thus designed to help poor comprehenders do just that, by enhancing their ability to consider multiple meanings at one time.

Instructional Activities

In this section I will describe research-tested activities that you can do with your word callers to foster a more flexible approach to text by helping them become more aware of multiple meanings. Yuill and Zipke and colleagues found that these activities are effective when taught in different lessons on different instructional days, rather than all together within one lesson. Thus, you might do each of these activities on separate instructional days or choose one activity on which to focus each week. Also, these activities are engaging and effective for more able readers, too.

Discussing and Generating Homonyms and Homophones

Begin this lesson by telling your students that sometimes words can sound the same but have different meanings. Explain that when words are spelled the same way and have different meanings, they are called *homonyms*. To introduce your first homonym, rely on children's prior knowledge to present the concept. Ask them if they know two meanings for the word *ball*. Usually, because they are familiar with the Cinderella story, children have heard *ball* used to refer to a dance. Further, they all have experience with basketballs, baseballs, and the like. Thus, you can guide discussion of the multiple meanings for *ball*, based on children's past experience. Other homonyms that might be familiar to your students include *bat* (baseball equipment or flying animal), *duck* (a quacking bird or the act of lowering oneself suddenly), and *gum* (a sticky substance we chew or a part of the mouth).

Next, explain that sometimes words can sound the same but have different spellings, and these are called *homophones*. (You might point out that the word part *-phone* reminds us of a telephone and lets us know that the words sound the same even if they aren't spelled alike.) To draw on your students' experience with a common homophone, ask them if they know what *night* means. Your students will undoubtedly talk about the time of day when it's dark outside. However, they are likely familiar with *knights*, too, the brave individuals who fought dragons. Guide your students' discussion so that they discover these two meanings. Other homophones that might be familiar to your students include *hare* (a rabbit) and *hair* (on our heads), *right* (correct or opposite of left) and *write* (the act of marking words on paper), *tale* (a story) and *tail* (an appendage on an animal), and *sea* (an ocean) and *see* (to visualize).

After you introduce homonyms and homophones, have your students generate as many homonyms and homophones as they can, and support them in this process by saying words and having the students think of the multiple meanings. See the resources at the end of this chapter for published lists of homophones and homonyms to help you with this task. To extend this activity you might have your students draw pictures of the different meanings of their homonyms or homophones. Or, you might have them write sentences with their homonym or homophone pairs, such as *I write with my right hand*, or *Cinderella tripped on a ball at the ball*. Save the lists your students generated in this lesson for a later activity on jokes and riddles.

Discussing and Generating Compound Words

This activity involves finding multiple meanings for compound words. Remind your students that compound words are long words made of smaller words, like *butterfly*, *bulldog*, or *eyeball*. Ask your students if they know what *butterfly* means.

This question will undoubtedly produce much commentary on the various kinds and colors of butterflies your students have encountered. Commend them for knowing the regular meaning of *butterfly*, and then, ask your students if they can think of another meaning for *butterfly*—a silly meaning. If they have trouble, give them a hint: tell them to think about the two little words that make up the word *butterfly*. If necessary, guide them to consider that *butterfly* could also mean a stick of butter with wings or a fly made of butter. Once your students have grasped the multiple potential meanings for *butterfly*, present another compound word with which your students have some familiarity, such as *eyeball*, and ask them to think of two meanings for that word. See the resources at the end of this chapter for published lists of compound words. Finally, have your students generate their own compound words with multiple meanings for each. Have them explain their choices. To extend the activity, you can have them draw pictures of the regular and silly meanings of one of the compounds they generated.

Looking Closely at Words

As I mentioned earlier, some struggling students benefit from learning how to pay attention to the internal structure of words because words' parts, or morphemes, provide important clues children can use to discover meaning. Take the word *discover*, for example, which is composed of *dis-* and *cover*. These separate parts can help students understand that *discover* means *to take the cover off of something*. This analysis requires that students understand the meaning of *cover*, but it also requires that they understand the meaning of the prefix *dis-*. Katz and Carlisle (2009) engaged struggling readers in several activities to increase their awareness of word parts, which can be easily implemented in your classroom. Each of these activities makes struggling readers more explicitly aware of the different kinds of parts found in words and how those parts affect meaning. (Consult *The Reading Teacher's Book of Lists* [Fry and Kress 2006] to find words appropriate for each of these activities; see the citation at the end of this chapter.)

- You can provide children lists of words with extra morphemes, such as *cats*, *fuzzy*, and *purred*, and have your students highlight the base words (*cat*, *fuzz*, and *purr*) to help them separate roots from affixes (e.g., prefixes, suffixes) and understand how each affects meaning.

- You can provide children lists of words with affixes and have them highlight the "fixes" (Katz and Carlisle 2009) by underlining all the affixes in the list.

- Students can sort words by morphological similarities. For example, words could be sorted into different piles according to similarity in roots' meanings, or words could be sorted by whether they have prefixes or suffixes, or students could sort by affixes' meanings.

- Another activity that helps students become aware of word parts' meanings is to give them a set of words that includes several words with the same morphemes, and then ask the students to come up with a definition for the words' parts. They might think of additional words with similar morphemes if they get stuck. For example, you might give your students the words *undo*, *unhappy*, *uncomfortable*, *return*, *remind*, and *redo*. Students would have to discover meanings for *un-* and *re-*.

- Finally, you can provide students with roots and morphemes on cards, which students can combine to create words of their own. You might add a bit of fun by asking students to create nonsense words and then require them to explain the new words' meanings based on their knowledge of word parts' meanings. For example, students might combine *dis-* and *help* to form *dishelp*, which might mean *to harm someone* or *to prevent someone from doing something*.

Discussing and Generating Ambiguous Sentences

Sometimes sentences are structured such that they can be interpreted in two ways. I presented such a sentence earlier in the chapter: *The keys were found by the dog*. This sentence could mean that the keys were located next to the dog, or it could mean that the dog found the keys. Ambiguous sentences such as this one provide another opportunity for children to practice thinking about multiple meanings in text. Write the sentence, *The keys were found by the dog*, on the board or on chart paper, and ask your students what it means. Alternatively, you can ask them to draw a picture of what the sentence means and ask them to share their drawings. Then, ask your students if the sentence can mean something else. Guide them to the correct answer if necessary. Write another sentence on the board, or distribute such sentences on handouts, and ask your students to find the meanings in the sentences. To extend the activity, you might have your students draw pictures of each of the alternate meanings for an ambiguous sentence, or you might have students try to generate their own ambiguous sentences (even if they are just variants of the ones you presented, such as *The toy was found by the baby*, which could mean that the toy was next to the baby or that the baby found the toy). Here are some ambiguous sentences to use for this activity. Additionally, in the resource section at the end of this chapter there is a website with ambiguous (and silly) headlines. Lynn Truss' (2006) children's version of *Eats, Shoots & Leaves* provides additional sentences appropriate for this lesson.

> The boy chased the dog on his bike. (Either the boy was riding, or the dog was riding.)
>
> The cow hit the farmer with the horn. (Either the cow hit the farmer with the cow's own horn, or the cow hit the farmer who was holding a horn.)
>
> Sally used the computer on the desk. (Either the computer was on the desk, or Sally was on the desk.)
>
> John ran into the house. (Either John ran inside the house—probably through a door—or John collided with the house.)
>
> I eat my pancakes with sausage. (Either I eat pancakes and sausage in the same meal, or I use sausage as a utensil to eat my pancakes.)

Discussing and Generating Jokes and Riddles

As noted earlier in the chapter, jokes and riddles that rely on ambiguous words provide a wonderful way for students to practice thinking about multiple meanings of text. As in the previous lessons, begin with a question for your students, but this time make the question a riddle, such as the newspaper riddle with which I introduced the chapter. Ask your students why the riddle is funny, and guide them to discover the multiple meanings of the homophones *red* and *read*. Explain that a riddle is a question, and its answer is silly because it has a different meaning than the one in the question. Discuss a few more riddles to ensure your students grasp the concept (see Figure 5–1 for examples). Explain to your students that they will be making their own riddles, and ask them for an example of a homonym or homophone. Scaffold their construction of a riddle. Extend the activity by having students use their homonym and homophone lists from a previous lesson to make riddles of their own, and ask the students to explain why the riddles are funny. Students' explanations should include both meanings of their ambiguous words. Consider this example of a teacher working with one student.

TEACHER: Can anybody tell me two meanings for the word *night*? (Note that children don't see the word, they only hear it, so spelling is irrelevant at this point.)

STUDENT: I know! It's like when it's dark outside, and knight can also be that guy who kills dragons!

TEACHER: Exactly! Well, today we're going to think of our own riddles, like the newspaper riddle. Remember, the newspaper riddle was tricky because the question sounded like it was talking about the color red, but the answer to the riddle was about when you read the newspaper—it was read all over! Riddles are tricky because they start with a question about one meaning, and then the answer is about a different meaning! Let's try to make a riddle about night. What can we ask about night?

STUDENT: Well, night comes after day, so we could ask what night comes after.

TEACHER: Good. That's a good start. So, now let's think about the other meaning for night. What do knights go after? What did you tell me about those people who are knights?

STUDENT: Oh, yeah! Knights go after dragons! They chase dragons. So, we could ask What does the night go after? Then, everybody's gonna think day. And, then we can say The knight goes after a DRAGON! (Laughs.)

TEACHER   (*Laughing*): That's a great riddle with a tricky answer. You're right. When you asked What does night go after?, that made me think about day, and then you surprised me with an answer that was about the other meaning for knight—the person who chases dragons! Good job using both meanings!

Zipke's (2008) *Reading Teacher* article provides additional description of the riddle generation process and is reprinted on the Reading Rockets website at the following web page: www.readingrockets.org/article/28315#meanings.

Exploring Multiple Meanings in Texts

Select a book, such as an Amelia Bedelia book, that permits discussion of multiple meanings to read aloud to your students (see the list in Figure 5–2). Prior to the lesson, read the book and list the instances in which Amelia Bedelia makes mistakes because she misinterprets ambiguous words or sentences. Before you read the story to your students, remind them (or explain to them, for children unfamiliar with the book series) that Amelia Bedelia makes many mistakes because she gets confused about the meanings of words. Then, as you read the text aloud to your students, have them raise their hands when they note one of Amelia's mistakes. Discuss each instance, provide relevant background knowledge if necessary (e.g., if your students do not know that *draw* can mean *open*), and have your students explain Amelia's mistakes, scaffolding their explanations to ensure that they grasp the multiple meanings in the ambiguous language that prompted the mistakes. Figure 5–2 includes many different texts that will work for this purpose.

More Ideas for Developing Wordplay and Awareness of Multiple Meanings

The research-tested activities in this chapter are fun, and they provide great ways for children to understand that words and texts can have multiple meanings. This section suggests other, related ways that you might promote this kind of word-play in your classroom.

Homophone Detectives

You might consider choosing a homophone (or homonym)-a-day to feature in your classroom. Tell your students the secret homophone each morning, and have your students "catch" you using the multiple forms of the daily homophone. Each time they catch you, they could write the appropriate form on the board or put a marble in a "homophone jar" to work toward earning a class prize. In upper grades you might designate a word sleuth each day to identify ambiguous words in class (e.g., in texts, in your speech or peers' speech, etc.) and make the sleuth responsible for adding the "discovered" words to the homophone/homonym list on the word wall or on the board.

Homophone Hangman

All students enjoy the classic game of hangman, in which players guess words letter by letter based on clues. Homophone hangman provides clues to both meanings for ambiguous words, with blanks for each form. For example, you might write the following clues on the board.

a bunny wig

___ ___ ___ ___   ___ ___ ___ ___

Have your students guess, letter by letter, according to the traditional hangman rules to find the correct answer (hare hair). Homophone hangman helps to make students aware of the multiple meanings and spellings for homophones.

Find the Fake

In this game, you should write homophones on the board (or on chart paper, the overhead projector, etc.) and include a nonword that, when pronounced, would sound the same as the words in the homophone set. For example, you might write these sets of words on the board.

there	their	thare
bear	bair	bare
chepe	cheap	cheep

Then, have your students find the fake words. In order to provide a correct answer, they must tell the meanings of the real forms and then identify the false form. Variations on this activity would permit the students to make up their own meanings for the fake forms or to generate their own sets of words, including a "fake" one (Make the Fake).

Silly Stories

To learn new vocabulary words, we often have children use the words in authentic writing assignments. This activity can be adapted to help your students master the multiple meanings of homophones. Have your students use homophone pairs (or multiple homophone pairs) to write silly stories that students can share with one another, fostering discussion of homophones to support understanding of multiple meanings. Or, you might combine your students' silly homophone stories into a book that can be placed in the classroom library. For younger students, a silly sentence with a picture would serve the same purpose. (I expect you will see many pictures of Aunt Ant and bare bears!)

Memory (Concentration)

Another way to help your students learn about homophones is to use the homophones (or their meanings) in a memory game, sometimes called concentration. This works well for buddy work or at a literacy center. Create cards with homophones on them, one word per card, so that you have several pairs or sets represented. Shuffle the cards and have the students lay them face down on a desk or table. Students take turns turning over pairs of cards to find homophone pairs. If a student finds a pair, he gets to keep the cards, and the student with the most pairs at the end of the game is the winner. This activity will help children recognize homophones in pairs or sets.

Remember, the coordination of multiple *meanings* in homophone sets is what helps students improve their flexible thinking, because they learn to think about each pronunciation in multiple ways. Thus, to help your students improve their focus on meanings in this activity you should create a second memory game with *only meanings* on the cards. Game play proceeds in the same manner, but students must match the meanings of words in a homophone pair. For example, "your parent's sister" and "a small bug" would be appropriate definitions for *aunt* and *ant*, respectively, and only the definitions should appear on the cards. This more advanced memory game assumes that your students already have knowledge of homophone pairs.

The following section includes additional resources you can use to find homonyms, homophones, compound words, ambiguous sentences, and riddles to support your instruction. For struggling comprehenders and able readers alike, all of the activities presented in this chapter can be fun. Wordplay motivates students to learn, and you can use these enjoyable activities to motivate flexible thinking about meaning in your students.

Resources for Teaching Children to Consider Multiple Meanings

Homonym Resources

www.enchantedlearning.com/english/homonyms/

www.funbrain.com/whichword/index.html

www.homonym.org/

Fry, Edward, and Jacqueline Kress. 2006. *The Reading Teacher's Book of Lists.* San Francisco: Jossey-Bass.

Compound Words Resources

www.enchantedlearning.com/grammar/compoundwords/

Fry, Edward, and Jacqueline Kress. 2006. *The Reading Teacher's Book of Lists.* San Francisco: Jossey-Bass.

Ambiguous Phrase Resources

www.fun-with-words.com/ambiguous_headlines.html

www.idiomsite.com/

Jokes and Riddles Resources

www.azkidsnet.com/riddles.htm

http://tiki.oneworld.net/fun/jokes/jokes.html

http://kids.niehs.nih.gov/jokes.htm#jokes

www.squiglysplayhouse.com/JokesAndRiddles/index.html

Fry, Edward, and Jacqueline Kress. 2006. *The Reading Teacher's Book of Lists.* San Francisco: Jossey-Bass.

How Does This Help You?

Questions to Consider

- Activities presented in this chapter promote play with language to support the development of word consciousness and comprehension. Identify three points in the instructional day in which this kind of wordplay might be naturally incorporated.

- Do you already have texts in your classroom library that include jokes, riddles, compound words, or ambiguous words or phrases? If so, how would you use these texts to increase your students' awareness of multiple word meanings? If not, look at the list in Figure 5–2 and consider which kinds of texts you might add to your classroom library and instructional routines to foster your students' awareness of multiple meanings.

A Picture Is Worth a Thousand Words

Pictorial and Verbal Activities

6

A couple of winters ago, I decided I was going to learn to knit. So, as any good reader would do, I bought a book (*The Cool Girl's Guide to Knitting: Everything the Novice Knitter Needs to Know*, by Nicki Trench [2005]), because I can, of course, learn just about anything from a book. (Or so I thought.) After I bought the book, I went to my local craft store and bought some festive, frizzy green yarn to make a scarf, and some nice fat knitting needles that my book said were perfect for a beginner. I figured a scarf couldn't be too hard. A rectangle: that was a simple shape. I was sure I could handle that. I curled up one evening with some tea, my new equipment, and my knitting book, with grand plans of starting my scarf. My first task was to figure out how to get that yarn onto those needles. I read about how to start. Then, I looked at the tiny pictures. Hmmm. I looked at my yarn, and I looked at my knitting needles. And, I reread the text and then relooked at the pictures. No dice. I just couldn't make the leap from the page to the equipment. My prior knowledge was skimpy, at best, and I just couldn't decipher what I found on those pages and coordinate all the new equipment and concepts. I needed to see what real knitting looked like. I needed additional, tangible support in order to construct meaning from that text. So, I went to my computer and Googled *knitting video*. The website www.knittinghelp.com was first on the list and sounded quite helpful (pun intended). I found a short video on that site, titled *Casting On*, which demystified the knitting process for me—at least I finally understood how to start! Several scarves later, I don't need the video to start, and the book makes a bit more sense to me. I chose this example to illustrate the importance—and occasional necessity—of tangible supports for struggling comprehenders. (Although I would generally consider myself to be in the skilled comprehender category, I definitely struggled to comprehend that knitting book.)

For many years we have heard of the importance of visualizing meaning to support reading comprehension (Pressley 1976). In fact, the more readers engage in sensory experiences related to meaning, the better their understanding of text (e.g., Block, Parris, and Whitely 2008; Wilhelm 2002). Why is this the case? Well, such activities help readers create a mental representation of—that is, an organized idea about—a text's meaning. With respect to my knitting book, an informational text, I needed additional support to help me organize and interpret what I found in its pages. Likewise, when readers visualize the events and characters in a fictional text, they are creating a mental picture of the text's meaning that they can use to support understanding of new text information as they continue to read. These kinds of visualization activities are natural for skilled readers (Sadoski 1985). Consider a recent conversation I had with one of my faculty colleagues—an experimental physicist (and a good comprehender)—in which he exclaimed, "Good readers are visual. When I read, it's like I'm watching TV in my head!" (Doughty 2009). Even though his expertise is not in reading, as a skilled comprehender he is well aware of the processes that good readers use automatically (Sadoski 1985). In addition to visualization of meaning, good readers may also construct verbal representations of texts' meanings in their minds—that is, verbally organized ideas about texts' meanings (Kintsch 1994). Either way, visual or verbal mental representations of texts' meanings are necessary for comprehension to occur.

This seems to be old news. Why did I include it in this book? Well, word callers may be less likely than their peers who are better comprehenders to engage in visualization of texts' meanings (also called mental imagery) while reading (Sadoski 1983, 1985). In fact, word callers are less likely than their peers to think about meaningful aspects of text in any manner, whether visual or verbal. (See Chapter 1 for more on word callers' difficulties processing meaning.) This means that these struggling comprehenders need extra support to be able to think about decoding and meaning at once, just as I needed extra support to construct meaning from my knitting text (e.g., Oakhill and Patel 1991). The purpose of this chapter is to share some research-tested techniques that are not widely known but have had particular success in helping struggling comprehenders construct meaning, resulting in improved reading comprehension for these students. (See Gersten et al. 2001; Martin and Duke in press; and Talbott, Lloyd, and Tankersley 1994, for reviews of research on comprehension interventions for struggling readers; also see Wanzek and Vaughn 2007 for a review of research on reading interventions, including comprehension interventions, for struggling learners.)

INSIGHT FROM CHILDREN'S THINKING

As we learned in Chapter 2, word callers define reading in terms of letters, sounds, and correct pronunciations, and they focus rather inflexibly on these aspects of texts, seemingly unable also to consider texts' meanings. Consequently, these students often need an extra push to make the break from text and shift their focus to meaning. Such a shift is necessary so that they can construct ideas about the meaning of texts, whether the ideas are visual or verbal. Further, comprehension requires that readers continually update their ideas about meaning while they read, which requires that they switch flexibly between decoding and meaning-making processes. Not surprisingly, instructional techniques that provide additional supports for meaning construction, such as the ones described in this chapter, produce significant improvements in word callers' comprehension. In particular, the techniques I share in this chapter focus on providing concrete supports that reduce the mental demands of meaning construction—just as the knitting video did for me—by making meaning visible to these struggling learners in tangible ways and enabling them to consider meaning alongside word-level aspects of print.

The Research Base

Many varieties of supports have been investigated for children who have difficulty focusing on meanings in text, but not all of these techniques have been made readily available for teachers who struggle with meeting word callers' needs. Thus, even though some of the research reviewed here was conducted several years ago, the research-tested instructional techniques are relevant for our current discussion because they are particularly effective for helping word callers construct meaning. As I noted earlier, for example, we have known for some time that imagery, also called *visualization*, is a powerful strategy for improving reading comprehension (Levin 1973; Pressley 1976) because it ensures that readers focus on meaning in addition to decoding processes. (Note that I use *imagery* and *visualization* interchangeably in this chapter to refer to the same process of making mental pictures of texts' meanings.) And, structured imagery instruction with pictorial supports has been successful in improving word callers' comprehension (Levin 1973; Oakhill and Patel 1991). Levin (1973), for example, taught fourth-grade word callers and skilled comprehenders in the midwestern United States to visualize texts' meanings to understand stories. He did this by showing the children pictures of events in stories and using those pictures to teach the children explicitly how to create *mental* pictures of meaning in texts. He found that visualization improved word callers' reading comprehension to such an extent that they scored as high as good comprehenders. Similarly, in a study of nine- to ten-year-old good and poor comprehenders in Brighton, England, Oakhill and Patel (1991) presented students with pictures of critical events in stories and then used those pictures to teach students to make mental images of texts' meanings, which improved word callers' comprehension. Expanding on this idea even further, Rubman and Waters (2000) developed a storyboard procedure, which reduced the cognitive demands of visualization even more by enabling third- and sixth-grade students to create a physical image of the text using magnetic cutouts of characters and setting. (Remember using flannel boards of characters and scenes in stories? The storyboards were similar to this activity.) In this study, skilled and less-skilled readers were taught to arrange cutout pictures of characters and objects on a magnetic board to depict important story content. Students who were taught to use the storyboards had significantly better comprehension than their peers who just read the stories, and the improvements were even greater for the struggling readers. Visualization training can also help improve comprehension even in very young children, as early as age seven (Borduin, Borduin, and Manley 1994; Center et al. 1999).

Visualization of events in stories provides one way to think about texts' meanings. However, mental models of texts' meanings can also be verbal, and some researchers have found that structured verbal representations of texts' meanings improve struggling readers' comprehension, too. Idol (1987; Idol and Croll 1987), for example, developed a story-mapping procedure to help struggling readers identify the important meaning components in a text by writing them in a simplified story map. Similarly, Jenkins et al. (1987) taught third- to sixth-grade struggling readers to build a meaning model for texts using paragraph restatements, and these verbal meaning-making techniques also improved struggling readers' comprehension. (I should note that story maps have also been shown to improve young readers' comprehension in children as early as first grade [Baumann and Bergeron 1993].) Many other kinds of verbal representations have been shown to enhance students' comprehension, such as using informational text structures, graphic organizers, and summaries. I won't discuss all of these different types in this chapter, but I encourage you to explore the benefits of other supports for meaning construction once you have mastered the techniques presented here.

Taken together, these studies show that word callers' comprehension can be improved by providing additional supports for meaning construction, whether they are visual or verbal. As I noted above, although the techniques presented in this chapter have been shown to be particularly effective for improving word callers' comprehension, they have not been widely shared with teachers who struggle with how to help word callers make the shift to more meaning-focused reading.

The Purpose of the Instructional Activities: Helping Word Callers Construct Meaning

Each of the instructional activities presented in this chapter provides extra, tangible support to help word callers break away from print and construct meaning from text in either visual or verbal form. Because word callers have difficulty constructing meaning on their own while decoding, these activities enable them to add meaning-making processes to their repertoires of reading processes so that they achieve better comprehension.

Instructional Activities

Scaffolded Imagery

Visualization can be taught effectively even to our youngest readers. For example, Brown et al. (1996) taught visualization to second-grade students in their year-long study of Transactional Strategies Instruction (see Chapter 8 for more on this instructional technique). And, more recently, Pilonieta and Medina (2009) taught visualization to first graders in their study of primary-grade comprehension instruction. I recall being in a first-grade classroom where the teacher told her students to "make movies in your mind when you read" to remind them to use the visualization strategy—a strategy they had clearly learned earlier in the year. Even though early elementary-aged children can learn to use the visualization strategy effectively, word callers may not always benefit from typical visualization instruction. When extra supports are provided, however, word callers can benefit as much as their peers. Here I will present two ways to support word callers' use of visualization: one-session sentence pictures, and three-session story pictures.

> *For these activities and other visualization activities,* texts without illustrations or those in which there is more content in the written words than in the illustrations are especially good for teaching visualization. Keep in mind that text from illustrated books can be retyped on plain paper to support this instruction.

One-Session Sentence Pictures

The first imagery activity, which is based on Levin's (1973) work, can be done in one individual or small-group lesson. For this activity, you should choose a short, illustrated story that can be divided into sentences. To prepare for the lesson, type the sentences on separate pages and combine them into a booklet. By dividing the story into smaller pieces, your students are only expected to think about one sentence at a time, which reduces the mental demands of the reading task and provides students a point to pause and make images before moving on to the next idea in the story. Before you give your students their booklets, tell them that they will be learning to think about the meanings of stories today. Explain that you are going to give them a story, divided into sentences. And then, explain that their job is to think of a picture for each sentence that they read. Give each child a booklet, and work with them on the first two sentences. To begin, read the first sentence with your students, and remind them that they should think of a picture for the sentence. After a few moments to think, discuss with your students what kinds of pictures they might make for the sentence. Work with them on the second sentence, and then, allow your students to work their way through the booklet, imagining pictures for each sentence as they go.

For example, consider the beginning of this lesson, based on the book, *The Lion and the Mouse*, by Cheyenne Cisco (1997).

TEACHER   (*To small group*): Today we're going to practice visualizing what's going on in a story. Good readers make pictures in their minds when they read, and it helps them understand and remember the story better. So, we're going to practice doing this together. Your booklets have sentences from a story called *The Lion and the Mouse* by Cheyenne Cisco. But, these sentences don't have pictures, because we're going to make them in our minds. Okay, let's look at the first sentence in your booklets. It says, "A big, bossy lion and a quiet, little mouse lived side by side in the jungle" (2).

The first page in your students' booklets should contain this sentence but no illustration. For the first sentence, ask your students what they visualized, and share your mental picture, too.

TEACHER: Everybody close your eyes and think about what that might look like, "A big, bossy lion and a quiet, little mouse lived side by side in the jungle" (2). Make a picture in your mind. (*Pause to allow students to visualize for a few moments*.) I'm thinking about a big, loud lion and a little, teeny mouse with trees all around. Okay, open your eyes. Does somebody want to share what their picture looks like?

You might hear descriptions of children's mental pictures, such as those that follow.

STUDENT 1:   The lion and the mouse sitting by each other. And, the lion's big: way bigger than the mouse.

STUDENT 2:   I see two houses for the lion and the mouse so they live by each other in the woods.

STUDENT 3:   I thought of a lion and a mouse.

Scaffold their understanding of the task, when necessary. For example, for the child who answered, "I thought of a lion and a mouse" you might want to ask,

"What are the lion and the mouse doing?" Or, "Where are the lion and the mouse? What do you see around them?" After you discuss possible pictures for the first sentence, present an illustration from the story to show your students what kind of picture they might consider for that sentence. Do the same scaffolded imagery instruction, supported with an actual illustration for the second sentence.

Once your students understand the task, allow them to do the visualization activity with less support. Stop occasionally to have your students share their mental pictures, and point out places where they might have missed important details. Consider this sentence from *The Lion and the Mouse* (7).

Bam! The lion's huge, hairy paw came down on the mouse's bald, pink tail.

You may elaborate on your students' mental pictures by noting things like, "Nice lion paw. Think back to the sentence, though. What did the lion have on his paws? Can you add those details?" or "What do you think the mouse's face looked like? Do you think he looked happy or scared?" Have your students continue to read the sentences in their booklets silently at their own pace, pausing to make mental pictures for each page, one sentence at a time. You can assess your students' comprehension of the story by asking questions about the story after they have finished reading and making pictures. You might extend the activity by having your students talk about their pictures or draw their favorite mental pictures from the lesson and describe what they show about the story. This lesson can be repeated with other stories on different instructional days if you find that your students need additional support for visualizing text content, although Levin (1973) showed that word callers' comprehension improved after work with only one story!

Three-Session Story Pictures

The second imagery activity is based on Oakhill and Patel's work with nine- to ten-year-olds (1991) and is a more intensive intervention that extends across three lessons on different days with small groups of struggling readers. Although visualizing text content supports comprehension, struggling comprehenders sometimes need even more explicit guidance in understanding story structure as a way to organize their mental pictures. Thus, in addition to helping students make mental pictures of stories' content, this instructional activity also helps children focus on story structure by (1) imagining the most important event in a story, (2) imagining the sequence of events in stories, and (3) using a strategy to picture and remember important details from stories. For this activity, you will need a few short stories, printed on single pages without illustrations, with copies for each of your students. These need not be long stories. The longer the story, the greater the memory demands on your students, and the purpose of these activities is to help your students visualize story structure, not have them wade through lengthy texts. You might choose to use the text from picture books, for example, typed on a single page, without illustrations. Even older students enjoy stories in picture books. Or, if you're feeling especially creative, you might write brief stories yourself. As with our first imagery activity, you should create some comprehension questions for each story to assess your students' understanding if you don't already have them.

For two of the stories you should create two drawings, which you will use on different instructional days: (1) a picture of the main event in the story, and (2) a four-picture sequence (like a cartoon panel) of the events in the story. So, for example, if you selected the nursery rhyme, "Jack and Jill," as one of your stories, you would create a picture of the main event (Jack and Jill on a hill with a pail of water, while Jack falls). And, you would also create a four-picture sequence of the events in the story that might include: Jack and Jill going up the hill carrying a pail, Jack and Jill getting water from a well at the top of the hill, Jack falling and spilling the water, and Jill rolling down the hill after Jack. For older students, you might choose a picture book, such as *Sock Monkey Goes to Hollywood* (Bell 2003). In this story, a very dirty sock monkey is nominated for an award, but in order to attend the award ceremonies in Hollywood, Sock Monkey must have a bath—a task he finds daunting, at best. So, Sock Monkey's friends help him with the bathing process, alleviating his fears; and he is able to attend the ceremonies, where he receives an award for "cleanest nominee." For this story, your main-event picture might depict a sparkly clean Sock Monkey traveling to Hollywood (via limousine), invitation in hand. Your four-picture sequence might include: a dirty sock monkey, Sock Monkey reading his award nomination, Sock Monkey getting a bath, and Sock Monkey receiving an award.

For the initial lesson on the first day, tell your students that they are going to learn to "think in pictures" when they read to help them remember stories better (Oakhill and Patel 1991, 112). Have your students read one of the short stories you selected. For the sake of example, I will continue with "Jack and Jill." Although this is a simple story, it will serve as a useful sample for how to implement the lesson. After they finish reading, present the main-event picture and explain that it is a *representational picture* because it represents facts in the story. For our sample story, the representational picture shows Jack, Jill, that they were carrying a pail of water, and that Jack fell. Explain that a representational picture like this one helps readers remember stories better because it helps them remember important facts. Then, share the four-picture cartoon sequence that you created to represent the sequence of important events in the story. Explain to your students how each of the four panels illustrates the order of events in the story: Jack and Jill going up, Jack and Jill getting water, Jack falling and spilling water, and Jill tumbling down the hill after Jack. After these explanations, tell your students that they should imagine the pictures in their own minds because they will use them to answer questions about the story. Put the pictures away, and ask some comprehension questions about the stories, making sure to discuss with your students how they used the mental pictures to help them answer the questions.

After you finish questioning your students on the first story, give them a new story to read and ask them to make mental pictures just like the ones you showed them: a picture that represents the main event in the story and a four-picture cartoon sequence that shows the order of events in the story. When they finish reading, ask them to describe the images they created while reading and provide feedback to enhance their image-making ability, such as

"That's a good picture to represent the main event in the story."

"You might want to include a _____ in your picture to help you remember _____."

"Did you see _____ in your picture?"

"Could you tell me what _____ looked like in your picture?"

On the second instructional day, you will introduce a new kind of image, a *transformational image*, which helps children remember specific story information. For example, to remember the name of a character named Mr. Green, I might imagine him dressed all in green or with green hair or skin. For this lesson you will need two more short stories, each printed on one page without pictures. For one of the stories you should create a transformational picture as an example in addition to the main-event and story-sequence pictures. You might consider using the text from picture books, such as the ones in the following list.

- *Caps for Sale* by Esphyr Slobodkina
- *Library Mouse* by Daniel Kirk
- *Max's Words* by Kate Banks
- *Skippyjon Jones and the Big Bones* by Judy Schachner (or any books from the Skippyjon Jones series)
- *Sylvester and the Magic Pebble* by William Steig
- *Tacky the Penguin* by Helen Lester (or any books from the Tacky series)

To begin the lesson, ask your students if they remember the kinds of mental pictures they learned last time (main-event pictures and four-picture cartoon sequences) and talk about why they are important. Then, explain that they are going to learn how to make another kind of picture today, a transformational picture. Tell your students that transformational pictures are sometimes silly pictures that we create to help us remember details from stories. Have your students read the first story you selected and ask them to make main-event pictures and sequence pictures while they read, just like last time. After they finish reading, discuss their main-event pictures and four-picture sequences, and produce your main-event and sequence pictures as examples. Then, show your students the picture of a transformational image that you created to remember a specific detail from the story and explain how it helps you remember. As a closing activity, give your students a new story and ask them to make all three kinds of pictures while they read: main-event, four-picture sequences, and transformational pictures. As in Lesson 1, ask your students questions about their pictures and provide feedback to improve their imaging ability.

For example, consider the transformational images this teacher created to help her remember details from *Max's Words* by Kate Banks. In this story, Max is a boy with two older brothers, Benjamin and Karl, who collect stamps and coins, respectively. Although Max wanted his brothers to share their collections, they refused. So, Max decided to begin his own collection; and he chose to collect words.

TEACHER (*To small group*): Today we're going to learn how to create another kind of mental picture to help us remember details from stories. Now, we just read *Max's Words*, and I know I might have a hard time remembering what Benjamin and Karl collected, so I decided to create silly mental pictures to help me remember. These kinds of pictures are called *transformational images* because we change or transform the story in some way to help us remember important details. To remember that Benjamin collected stamps, I thought about a picture of Benjamin with a stamp-shaped head! And, to remember that Karl collected coins, what do you think I imagined?

STUDENT (*Laughs*): Karl with a coin-shaped head?

TEACHER: That's exactly right! I imagined Karl with a coin-shaped head. These silly transformational images will help me remember what Benjamin and Karl collected. You can make transformational images, too, when you read stories, so that you remember important details about what you're reading.

Finally, on the third instructional day, you will remind the students of the kinds of mental pictures they have learned to make and discuss how the pictures help us remember information in stories. Then, give your students a new story to read and ask them to make images while they do so. As in Lessons 1 and 2, after the students finish reading, discuss your students' images and provide feedback.

Storyboards

This is a more intensive individual intervention for students who have difficulty representing story content. This lesson involves a storyboard-making procedure to provide a tangible representation of stories' content to assist struggling comprehenders in meaning construction while reading (Rubman and Waters 2000). Although this activity was originally done with individual children, you could adapt it for work with small groups. For this activity you will need to select a story for the lesson and create cutouts of characters and important story elements to which you should affix magnets. (Sticky magnet strips would work well for this purpose.) You will also need a metal board (such as a large cookie sheet) on which students can place the magnetic cutouts. (A flannel board and Velcro figures or reusable stickers and a whiteboard would also work, depending on the resources you have available.) Explain to your student(s) that they are going to make a picture of the story while they read, using the characters and storyboard provided. After your student(s) finish, ask them to tell you about the story using the storyboard they made. To extend the activity, you might have the students create their own cutouts for stories. To support the development of students' imagery ability, you might discuss with them how good readers make storyboards in their heads.

Story Maps

To help struggling readers identify the important meaning components in a story, Idol (1987) developed a story-mapping activity with comprehension questions that can be used with any story. This activity should be completed across three lessons on different days in small-group or whole-group instruction. (If you choose to do this activity in whole-group instruction, you may want to use an overhead projector or reproduce the questions and story map on chart paper.) For each day of this activity, you will need the comprehension questions listed in Figure 6–1 with handouts for your students (adapted from Idol 1987), and you will need to create story map handouts for your students (see Figure 6–2 for the story map, reprinted from Idol 1987).

For the first lesson, explain to your students that they are going to learn how to use a story map to help them remember information about stories. Show them the ten comprehension questions in Figure 6–1, briefly explain each question, and tell your students that the story map will help them remember the answers to those questions. Have your students read a story, then distribute story maps to the students. While students fill in their own maps, you should complete a group map (displayed on an overhead projector or chart paper for a large group), calling on individual students to help fill in each portion of the story map as you go. Make sure each student has the opportunity to respond. Once the story map is complete, collect the individual story maps and have your students answer the ten comprehension questions independently. For example, if you chose to use *Ruby's Wish* by Shirin Yim Bridges for this activity, your group responses to the questions might look like those in Figure 6–3, and your group story map might look like that in Figure 6–4.

For the second lesson, use a new story and have your students fill in the story map independently. Tell them that they can complete the story map while they are reading or after they are finished. (Most students choose to complete the map after they read.) After the individual story maps are complete, complete a group story map (displayed on an overhead projector or chart paper for a larger group), calling on individual students to complete portions of the map. Collect the individual story maps and have students complete the ten comprehension questions independently.

In the third and subsequent lessons with new stories each time, students should complete story maps independently. Completion of a group story map is no longer necessary. After your students' first attempt at independent story maps, you may wish to have a small-group discussion of their maps to resolve confusions and reinforce appropriate responses.

FIGURE 6–1

Story Map Question Guide

NAME: _____ DATE: _____

1. Who were the main characters?

2. Were there any other important characters? Who?

3. When did the story take place?

4. Where did the story take place?

5. What was the problem in the story?

6. How did _____ try to solve the problem?

7. Was it hard to solve the problem? Explain.

8. Was the problem solved? Explain.

9. What did you learn from reading this story?

10. Can you think of a different ending?

FIGURE 6–2

Story Map

My Story Map

NAME _____ DATE _____

THE SETTING
CHARACTERS: TIME: PLACE:

THE PROBLEM

THE GOAL

ACTION

THE OUTCOME

FIGURE 6–3

Group Story Map Question Guide Responses for *Ruby's Wish*

1. Who were the main characters? Ruby and her grandfather

2. Were there any other important characters? Who? The teacher, other boys and girls, and the children's mothers

3. When did the story take place? A long time ago

4. Where did the story take place? In China

5. What was the problem in the story? Ruby was a good student but girls were expected to get married and were not allowed to go to University. Ruby did not think girls were treated fairly.

6. How did ___Ruby___ try to solve the problem? She studied hard, and she wrote a poem about how boys were treated better than girls.

7. Was it hard to solve the problem? Explain. No, she talked with her grandfather and he listened.

8. Was the problem solved? Explain. Yes, her grandfather helped her go to the University.

9. What did you learn from reading this story? A long time ago in China, girls were expected to get married and not go to college. Talking about problems will help find solutions.

10. Can you think of a different ending? Ruby's grandfather might have told her that she must get married and not go to University. That would have made her very sad.

FIGURE 6–4

Group Story Map Responses for *Ruby's Wish*

My Story Map

NAME Class Map - Ruby's Wish   DATE October 14

THE SETTING

CHARACTERS: TIME: PLACE:

Ruby, grandfather   A long time ago   China

Children, mothers

THE PROBLEM
Ruby was a good student, but girls were expected to get married and were not allowed to go to University.

THE GOAL
Ruby didn't think girls were treated fairly. She wanted to keep studying and go to University.

ACTION
Ruby studied hard and did well. She wrote a poem about how girls were not treated fairly, and she talked about it with her grandfather.

THE OUTCOME
Ruby's grandfather listened and he helped her go to University.

Paragraph Restatements

This activity is designed to help third- to fifth-grade students remember the most important ideas in a text by creating restatements of the most important people and events in each paragraph (Jenkins et al. 1987). For this small-group activity, you will need to retype stories (or passages) with blank lines printed between each paragraph. (Students will write their paragraph restatements on these lines.) This activity occurs in three phases across multiple days, and each phase should continue until children reach the criterion of 80 percent correct responses. (In the original research on this strategy, each instructional phase lasted from three to five days.)

1. *Modeling*. In the first phase, you should scaffold students' creation of restatements through modeling and feedback. Explain to your students that today they will learn how to choose the most important ideas in paragraphs to help them remember stories better. Provide students copies of the printed stories (or passages) you prepared with blank lines between paragraphs, and tell them to read the first paragraph. After they finish ask them two questions to support creation of restatements: "Who?" and "What happened?" (Jenkins et al. 1987, 55). If students do not respond to the questions, have them reread the paragraph. If they identify irrelevant or unimportant details, ask them "Was that the most important thing that happened in the paragraph?" (Jenkins et al. 1987, 55). Write students' restatements on the chalkboard, a whiteboard, or on chart paper so that the group can see them. Continue through the subsequent paragraphs, modeling the procedure and providing feedback as needed. Repeat the activity in subsequent lessons until students are able to provide approximately 80 percent correct responses.

2. *Student Practice.* The goal of the second phase is for students to understand that the best restatements should be as brief as possible (about three or four words) but still capture the gist of the main event in the paragraph. Provide students another printed story (or passage) with blank lines printed between paragraphs, and have students write restatements individually. Provide feedback individually to students when necessary. When students have finished their restatements, remove the passages, read some of the restatements aloud to the students, and have them recall the paragraph contents. This component permits students to evaluate whether their restatements provide enough information to remember the stories. This phase should continue, on different days if necessary, until students provide approximately 80 percent correct responses.

3. *More Independent Student Practice.* In the third and final phase, provide students stories (or passages) without lines between paragraphs. Explain to the students that instead of writing the restatements in the passages, they can write restatements on a separate sheet of paper to remember anything that

they read. Model the process with one or two restatements, and then permit the students to practice on their own. Continue this phase until students provide approximately 80 percent correct responses.

Closing Notes

To return to an important point from earlier in the chapter, the instructional techniques presented here have been identified through research as particularly successful in helping word callers achieve better reading comprehension. You may wonder what is special about these techniques and whether other graphic organizers might also help your struggling comprehenders. As you might have noticed, each technique in this chapter provides structured, specific, and scaffolded support for meaning construction that reduces the mental demands on word callers, who often have difficulty coordinating mentally all of the necessary components for successful comprehension. To think of this another way, word callers' mental space for reading processes is limited by their inflexibility, and instructional techniques must be sensitive to this particular need. To provide support that addresses this issue, each of the techniques presented in this chapter makes meaning visible or tangible in various ways, and most of these techniques scaffold students' knowledge of meaning construction slowly, over time, in order not to overload word callers' limited mental capacity. Other graphic organizers may certainly provide similar support to the techniques we discussed here, but we must be careful that the organizer strategies themselves do not overwhelm struggling comprehenders by using precious mental space that is needed for meaning construction.

How Does This Help You?

Questions to Consider

- Have you noticed that any of your students have difficulty remembering the important details or main ideas from texts? What techniques have you tried to help your students with this difficulty? Did these techniques work? Why or why not?

- What have you learned in this chapter that you might use to supplement your regular instruction for children who have trouble constructing meaning from text?

- This chapter presents two kinds of supports for meaning construction: visual and verbal. Think about your students who may vary in their optimal learning modality—some may be visual learners, while others may be auditory learners. Which of your students would benefit most from visual supports, and which would benefit from verbal supports?

7

Connecting the Dots

Lessons That Help Word Callers Infer

This chapter is about inference making, which is a bit like the connect-the-dots activities we completed as children. Remember how, once all the dots on a page were connected, a new picture emerged? Well, inference making operates in a similar fashion in that the connections made by readers—between different text concepts or between text concepts and readers' own knowledge—result in the emergence of new ideas that were not explicitly stated in the text. (Of course, connect-the-dots activities also required us to make connections in a particular, prescribed order, which is *not* the case for good inference making.)

In fact, authors *expect* readers to make inferences because they cannot possibly include all ideas or concepts that are relevant to a particular text's topic. That would be quite tedious for readers (as well as for writers). Further, authors assume that readers bring certain knowledge to texts, just as I assumed you were knowledgeable about connect-the-dots activities when I wrote the opening to this chapter. That is the beauty of the comprehension process. Good readers actively construct meaning—meaning that is not explicitly stated in text—by weaving details provided by the author with their own, personal knowledge and interpretations. Thus, each individual reader may weave a different tapestry from a particular text, because each reader's knowledge and experience commingle with text in a slightly different way. In a general sense, reading *is* inferring, and inferring is the most critical of all the comprehension strategies. However, as we learned in Chapter 1, poor comprehenders have particular difficulty making inferences, which is likely related to their inflexible focus on single ideas or text features at a time. Because inference making requires readers to coordinate and connect *multiple*, meaningful idea units, word callers have difficulty accomplishing this task.

To illustrate the process of inference making, consider this conversation I had with Sophie, a rising third grader and a good comprehender, who had just read a short story I wrote to test and teach inference making, titled "John and Skippy" (we will return to the "John and Skippy" story later in the chapter). Keep in mind that these questions were asked as part of an assessment. (Normally, I would ask more open-ended questions and engage children in a richer discussion about a text.) Note that each of my questions requires an answer that is not explicitly stated in the story. So, to answer correctly, Sophie had to make inferences. Here is the actual text of the story that Sophie read:

John, a first grader, rides the school bus every afternoon, and he is dropped off at the end of his driveway. Every day when John arrives home, Skippy greets him at the door with happy barking, and his mother has a snack ready for him. Sometimes John shares his snack with Skippy! When John arrived home from school yesterday, he walked up his driveway, climbed the three front steps, and opened the front door. Then, he quickly threw his backpack on the porch and called, "Skippy, come back! Bring back my cookies!," and he ran across the front yard as fast as he could.

Good comprehenders are able to read a story like this one and connect the important text components and prior knowledge to construct multiple understandings about the text. Before you consider my conversation with Sophie, take a look at the following list of ideas. Even though they were not explicitly stated in the story, you probably inferred that:

1. The school bus drops John at the end of his driveway every afternoon.
2. Skippy is John's dog.
3. John's mother makes a snack for John every day after school.
4. John rode the school bus home yesterday.
5. John lives in a house with a front porch and three front steps.
6. Even though he usually goes inside when he gets home, John ran across his front yard yesterday because he was chasing Skippy the dog, who must have escaped when John opened the front door.
7. John's mother made John cookies for his after-school snack yesterday.
8. Skippy swiped John's cookies before running out the front door!

After Sophie read the story about John and Skippy we had the following conversation. Note the inferences Sophie made in response to my questions.

ME: I've got a few questions about the story you just read, okay? Here's the first one. Where does the school bus drop John every day?

SOPHIE: At his driveway.

ME: Right! Who does Mom make a snack for after school?

SOPHIE: For him. For John.

ME: Yes! What is Skippy?

SOPHIE   (*Confidently*): Skippy is John's dog.

ME:	Good job! The story didn't actually tell you that! How did John get home from school yesterday?
SOPHIE:	He rode the school bus.
ME:	Right. What did John's mother make for a snack yesterday?
SOPHIE:	Ummm (*Slight pause while she thought a bit*) . . . cookies!
ME:	Good job! So, why did John run across the yard when he got home yesterday instead of going inside?
SOPHIE:	Because Skippy took the cookies.
ME:	Yes! I've got one more question for you. What did Skippy do yesterday when John got home?
SOPHIE:	He took the cookies and ran across the yard.
ME:	Terrific! You did a really good job with these questions. Lots of kids have a hard time with questions like these because the story doesn't actually tell you the answers. You have to figure them out. You did a great job with that because you are such a great reader!
SOPHIE:	Thank you!

Successful comprehenders like Sophie typically make two kinds of inferences when they read, text-connecting inferences and gap-filling inferences; these terms were conceived by Cain and Oakhill (1999), based on work by Baker and Stein (1981). I will continue to use this terminology in the current chapter, because it aptly describes the kinds of actions required of good inference makers. Both types of inferences require readers to connect pieces of information in order to construct ideas that are not explicitly presented in a text. In particular, a text-connecting inference is one in which a reader connects two bits of information from a text to construct an idea that is not explicitly stated. For example, in these sentences, *Manx cats have no tails. Keegan is a Manx cat.*, a good comprehender would infer that Keegan has no tail, even though the text does not explicitly state that idea. (Note: Keegan is *my* Manx cat, and he does, in fact, have no tail.) You likely made text-connecting inferences about John and Skippy. See items 1, 3, 4, and 7 in the list of inferences on page 95. The second type of inference, a gap-filling inference, requires that readers connect their own background knowledge to text information to construct meaning. Thus, after reading the following sentence, *Sarah forgot her umbrella this morning, and she got soaking wet today!*, a good comprehender would infer that it rained today even though the text never said that it rained. This inference requires that readers connect text information to important background knowledge about the purpose of umbrellas and the consequences that occur if an umbrella is not used on a rainy day. You made gap-filling inferences about John and Skippy, too. See items 2, 5, 6, and 8 in the list of inferences on page 95.

As I have worked with elementary school teachers on comprehension strategies instruction, I have found that inference making is one of the most difficult strategies to teach, and it is also one of the most difficult strategies for students to understand. These difficulties may stem from the fact that teaching inference making requires that we think about—and talk about—things that are not actually present in text. (It's much easier to talk about things that *are* there than to talk about things that are *not* there.) And, what's more, inference making requires that readers coordinate multiple ideas to construct valid inferences. For example, text-connecting inferences require readers to consider and coordinate two ideas presented in text, whereas gap-filling inferences require readers to consider and coordinate text ideas with prior knowledge. In both cases, readers must be able to consider two ideas at once and flexibly use them to construct new thoughts. Poor comprehenders, however, tend to be less flexible in their thinking and are significantly less likely than their peers with better comprehension to make inferences while reading (Laing and Kamhi 2002; Oakhill, Yuill, and Parkin 1986). Fortunately, some supportive inference-training interventions have been developed, which produce gains in word callers' inference making and reading comprehension (e.g., Carr, Dewitz, and Patberg 1983; McGee and Johnson 2003; Yuill and Joscelyne 1988; Yuill and Oakhill 1988), and these will be described later in this chapter.

INSIGHT FROM CHILDREN'S THINKING

Inference making requires that readers consider and connect multiple ideas, whether those connections are between ideas in a text or between the text and the readers' prior knowledge. As we learned in Chapter 2, because word callers have difficulty considering multiple ideas at once and coordinating them flexibly while engaging in tasks, these children have difficulty juggling and connecting the multiple ideas necessary for meaningful inference making. Further, because word callers tend to think about reading as a decoding task, they have difficulty shifting their thinking to the more meaning-focused ideas required for inference making.

The Research Base

Although children develop an awareness of inferences as a source of knowledge in oral language comprehension as early as four to five years of age (Keenan, Ruffman, and Olson 1994), constructing inferences from text is a more complex matter (Graesser, Singer, and Trabasso 1994). As noted in Chapter 1, children with poor reading comprehension have more difficulty making inferences than their peers with better comprehension (Cain and Oakhill 1999; Laing and Kamhi 2002). And, this difference does not appear to be due to memory (Oakhill, Yuill, and Parkin 1986; Cain and Oakhill 1999), general knowledge (Cain and Oakhill 1999), or to the degree of automaticity in children's decoding skill (Yuill and Oakhill 1988). However, the differences between good and poor comprehenders' inference-making skills are broad: word callers have more difficulty than good comprehenders inferring word meanings from context (Oakhill 1983), making text-connecting inferences (Oakhill 1982), and making gap-filling inferences (Oakhill 1984). If encouraged to look back at a text, word callers can make text-connecting inferences almost as well as their peers with better comprehension, but looking back does not improve their gap-filling inference performance (Cain and Oakhill 1999). This makes sense, as looking back makes both ideas to be connected in a text-connecting inference visible to readers (because two ideas are actually present in text). Thus, looking back provides tangible support for constructing meaning via text-connecting inferences. However, with gap-filling inferences, children must connect their own prior knowledge to text concepts, and looking back doesn't make children's own knowledge any more visible than it was the first time they read the text. Thus, children need other kinds of supports to make gap-filling inferences. Word callers' lack of inference-making skill is so pervasive that some researchers have suggested it is one of the candidate causes of their comprehension difficulties (Cain and Oakhill 1999). The good news is that inference making can be taught successfully to poor comprehenders, resulting in improvements in their inference-making ability and reading comprehension.

Interventions designed to teach inference-making skills have focused on both text-connecting and gap-filling inferences (McGee and Johnson 2003; Yuill and Joscelyne 1988; Yuill and Oakhill 1988), in which children learned to look for information in text to find clues to text meaning. Other interventions have focused more exclusively on gap-filling inferences, in which students learned to connect prior knowledge to text, because poor comprehenders seem to find these kinds of inferences particularly difficult (Carr, Dewitz, and Patberg 1983; Hansen and Pearson 1983). In each of these intervention studies, poor comprehenders demonstrated marked improvements in inference making and comprehension after training, often improving to the level of good comprehenders. In contrast, the children who were already skilled comprehenders did not demonstrate significant growth in comprehension and inference making. Because the poor comprehenders benefited more from the interventions than good comprehenders, researchers have surmised that teaching inference making supplies an important comprehension skill that word callers lack.

The Purpose of the Lessons: Coordinating Multiple Ideas While Reading

The instructional activities presented in this chapter are designed to make students aware that there are hidden meanings in text that must be discovered by making connections between different ideas in text or between text concepts and their own knowledge. Essentially, inference training helps to refocus word callers' attention on meaningful aspects of text. Additionally, because word callers have difficulty considering multiple ideas at once, the inference-making lessons provide scaffolded support and practice in doing so by requiring them to connect multiple ideas in text or coordinate text concepts with prior knowledge to construct new insights.

Instructional Activities

As noted previously, both text-connecting and gap-filling inference making can be taught, resulting in improvements in word callers' reading comprehension. In the following sections I describe research-tested instructional techniques to teach each of these types of inference making that have been used successfully to improve word callers' performance. The first technique is designed to support children's ability to make gap-filling inferences, using experiences from their own lives.

Connecting Lives to Stories

Connecting Lives to Stories is a series of two lessons in which students learn to make gap-filling inferences by connecting their own experiences to texts (Hansen 1981; Hansen and Pearson 1983). Poor comprehenders do not automatically make connections from texts to their own lives because they are typically focusing on decoding processes (Yuill and Oakhill 1991). To make gap-filling inferences, they must consider texts' meanings and their own experiences while also engaging in the decoding process. The lesson activities provide opportunities to practice these skills in small-group discussion, and they can be adapted for any story—even those in your basal reader. These lessons typically occur twice a week for ten weeks. The original work with these lessons used the ten stories (one per week) that the students were assigned from their basal readers (Hansen and Pearson 1983).

To prepare for your first week, select a story and determine which information might be familiar to your students. Then, on the first day you should introduce the story to your students and engage them in a discussion of their own experiences related to the story. For the second lesson you will need to prepare eight to ten questions that require students to consider information outside the text. That is, these questions should force students to rely on prior knowledge to formulate answers. Then, on the second day, after the students have read the story, engage them in a discussion of the inferential questions you prepared in advance. You may adapt these lessons by having students write about their life experiences and predictions in the first lesson and their inferential responses to your questions in the second lesson.

Consider this example, based on a story titled *Lucky Boy*, by Susan Boase (2002), which is about a lonely little brown dog called Boy, whose busy family does not have time for him. Boy's neighbor, whom he does not yet know, receives sympathy cards from the mailman and lives alone. (We infer that he has recently lost a spouse.) One day Boy digs under the fence, right into the neighbor's yard, and they form a wonderful friendship. In preparing a Connecting Lives to Stories lesson on *Lucky Boy*, I identified the concepts of friendship, loneliness, and dog ownership that might be familiar to elementary students.

- To introduce the first Connecting Lives to Stories lesson, explain, "I am going to tell you something that you can do before you read stories that will help you remember them better. Thinking about your own lives will help you make guesses (or predictions) about stories, which will help you understand them and remember them." (After the first lesson, continue to remind students of the purpose of the activity: "Do you remember what we should do before we read stories to help us remember them better? That's right, we should think about things in our own lives that are related to the stories.")

- In the first lesson on *Lucky Boy*, tell students that there are some important ideas in this story: friendship, loneliness, and having a dog. Then, ask them if they have ever felt lonely. Scaffold their understanding of loneliness to provide the basis for understanding Boy's and the neighbor's lonely feelings in the story. Do the same for friendship and for owning a dog. Hearing other students talk about their experiences provides each individual child a broader basis from which to make inferences when reading the story. Then, ask the students what they think the story might be about. A good first question is: "Why do you think the book is called *Lucky Boy*?"

- At the beginning of the second lesson, have your students read the story. (You may decide to read aloud or do a choral reading.) Remind your students of the discussion of their own lives in the last lesson. Then, present one of the inferential questions you prepared for this purpose. For example, my first question about *Lucky Boy* follows, along with a sample of student discussion.

ME: The story says that Boy "didn't start out lucky." Why do you think the story said that?

STUDENT 1: Because his family was too busy for him.

(Student 1's response is literal—it reiterates information already in the text; thus I scaffold an inference.)

ME: Why does having a busy family make Boy unlucky?

STUDENT 2: He's all by himself, so he's lonely! Like what we talked about before. His family doesn't have time to spend with him. So, he feels like he's by himself and nobody cares.

At this point you might remind students of their comments regarding loneliness in the last lesson to facilitate their Lives to Stories connections. Continue the discussion, posing inferential questions throughout the lesson to facilitate students' practice with gap-filling inferences—coordinating prior knowledge with text information. When you begin a new series of lessons with a new story in the following week, you should remind your students of this trick—*thinking about their own lives to remember stories*. Once your students understand the strategy, you can incorporate it into other instructional formats: whole-group discussion before read-alouds, or in individual work with struggling students. You might also consider having students write about prior experiences in preparation for reading stories. To ensure that students still retain the benefit of hearing about others' experiences, you can have students share journal entries with the group or class.

Two-Story Clue Hunt

This lesson is designed for work with individual students and is based on research by Yuill and Joscelyne (1988) to help children discover text-connecting and gap-filling inferences. Find a quiet table where you can work one-to-one with a student, perhaps while other students are at literacy centers or engaged in independent reading. In this lesson you will model the inference making with one story, and then you will have your student practice the same inference making technique on another story. In Figure 7–1, I have provided the "John and Skippy" story (from the beginning of this chapter), which can be used to teach the task, and a second story, "Mary's Birthday Present," to provide students an opportunity for practice. The inferences that can be made from each story are also printed in Figure 7–1. Text-connecting inferences are designated with a *T*, and gap-filling inferences are designated with a *G*. You can adapt this technique for use with any story by finding clue words within the story that help students discover inferences. I will use "John and Skippy" to illustrate the lesson procedure.

- To begin the lesson, tell your student, "Today you will learn to solve puzzles in stories. Sometimes stories don't tell us everything we need to know to understand them. I'm going to tell you a secret that will help you figure out the puzzles in stories."

- Tell your student that "the stories don't actually say exactly what's happening, but they give you some clues. You must look for the clues and make some guesses about what is going on. First we can practice together" (Yuill and Joscelyne 1988, 156).

- Give your student the "John and Skippy" story and provide sufficient time for him or her to read it.

FIGURE 7–1

Stories to Support Inference-Making Lessons

John and Skippy

John, a first grader, rides the school bus every afternoon, and he is dropped off at the end of his driveway. Every day when John arrives home, Skippy greets him at the door with happy barking, and his mother has a snack ready for him. Sometimes John shares his snack with Skippy! When John arrived home from school yesterday, he walked up his driveway, climbed the three front steps, and opened the front door. Then, he quickly threw his backpack on the porch and called, "Skippy, come back! Bring back my cookies!," and he ran across the front yard as fast as he could.

Inferences

1. The school bus drops John at the end of his driveway every afternoon. T

2. Skippy is John's dog. G

3. John's mother makes a snack for John every day after school. T

4. John rode the school bus home yesterday. T

5. John lives in a house with a front porch and three front steps. G

6. Even though he usually goes inside when he gets home, John ran across his front yard yesterday because he was chasing Skippy the dog, who must have escaped when John opened the front door. G

7. John's mother made John cookies for his after-school snack yesterday. T

8. Skippy swiped John's cookies before running out the front door! G

Mary's Birthday Present

It was Mary's birthday. She was wearing a party dress. Her friends came to her house, and they had cake and ice cream. There were six candles on the cake. Sam gave Mary a new toy for her birthday. Mary wanted to try it on the water. She went to the pond in her yard. It was a windy day. The wind blew the sail. "Oh, no!" said Mary. "My new boat is going too far!" Mary ran along the side of the pond and reached for the boat. "Oh, no!" Mary cried as she climbed onto the grass. "What will Mother say about my dress?"

"It's okay," said Mother. "Your dress will dry."

Inferences

1. Mary was having a birthday party. T

2. Mary is six years old. G

3. Sam gave Mary a toy sailboat for her birthday. T

4. Mary put the sailboat in the pond in her yard. G

5. The wind blew the sailboat too far. T

6. Mary couldn't reach the boat. T

7. Mary fell in the pond. G

8. Mary's party dress was wet. G

- After your student finishes reading the story, explain that "the puzzle in this story is about what John was doing yesterday and why John ran across the yard. That's what we need to figure out."

- Then, work through the following sets of clues. For each set, identify the clue words, and explain what the clues reveal about the story.

  1. *School bus*, *home*, *dropped off*, *driveway*, *door*, *front steps*, *front door*, *porch*, and *yard* are clues. Ask what your student thinks these clues tell us about the story. Explain that these clues tell us where John was. He came home from school on the bus, and he lives in a house (with a driveway, three steps, a front porch, and a yard). John walked up to his house after getting off the bus. Sophie used these clues to infer that the school bus dropped John at his driveway.

  2. *Mother*, *snack*, *ready*, and *cookies* are clues. These tell us that John's mother makes him a snack every day, and she made cookies for his snack yesterday. After thinking for a moment, Sophie connected these clues and realized that John's mother made him cookies yesterday.

  3. *Skippy*, *barking*, and *shares his snack* are clues. They tell us that Skippy is a dog who gets to eat some of John's snack sometimes! Sophie was confident in her inference that Skippy was John's dog.

  4. What John shouts is another clue, "*Skippy, come back! Bring back my cookies!*" along with *ran across the front yard*. These clues tell us that Skippy took John's cookies (probably because he is used to sharing with John), and John chased him across the yard. Sophie was able to connect these dots and successfully inferred that John was chasing Skippy, the cookie thief, across the yard.

- After you work through the first story, give your student another story and ask him or her to find the clue words and explain them to you. You should add any clues that your student does not mention and work with your student to develop an explanation for them. In "Mary's Birthday Present" (in Figure 7–1), your student might find these clues.

  1. *Birthday*, *party dress*, *friends*, *cake*, and *ice cream* are clues. They tell us that Mary is having a birthday party.

  2. *Birthday*, *cake*, *six*, and *candles* are clues. They tell us that Mary is six years old.

  3. *Toy*, *water*, *pond*, *wind*, *sail*, and *boat* are clues. They tell us that Sam gave Mary a toy sailboat.

  4. *Try it on the water*, *pond*, *yard*, and *ran along the side of the pond* are clues. They tell us that Mary put her new toy boat in the pond in her yard.

  5. *Wind*, *sail*, *boat*, *far*, and *reached for the boat* are clues. These tell us that the wind blew the toy sailboat too far away from Mary.

  6. *Reached for the boat*, "*Oh, no!*," *climbed onto the grass*, "*What will Mother say about my dress?*," and "*Your dress will dry*" are clues. They tell us that Mary fell into the pond and got her party dress all wet.

Although this lesson was developed for use with individual students, it can be adapted for small-group instruction by working on clue finding in group discussion. Once you have taught the technique to your students, you can ask them to find clues in any story and in multiple instructional formats, such as small-group or whole-group instruction. You might also adapt the technique for a literacy center by providing printed copies of short stories in which your students can highlight and explain story clues. This activity would also lead naturally into a journal-writing activity in which students write the clues they find and then write a sentence or two about their inferences (or solutions to the stories' puzzles).

Why might this activity be effective for these students? Research shows that it works, but this seems so simple to us as good comprehenders. Remember that word callers are typically quite focused on word recognition processes, and they seem to lack awareness that readers should even look for meanings in texts. Some children may need a bit of a nudge to shift their focus to meaning, and other children may need us to redefine the nature of the reading task as a meaning-seeking activity. This clue-finding lesson makes the hunt for meaning explicit for these children. They see texts with new eyes, and instead of looking at them as words to decode, they look at texts as meaningful puzzles to be solved.

Three-Step Inference Building: Six Small-Group Lessons

Another technique that is useful for improving word callers' inference-making skills is a more intensive three-step process that builds inference-making ability across a series of six or seven small-group lessons (McGee and Johnson 2003; Yuill and Oakhill 1988). Small groups should include approximately five students and meet twice per week. Thus, the entire intervention takes three to four weeks to complete. To start, I will describe the three steps of the lesson series, and after that I will provide a blueprint for the series of lessons, indicating when each of the three steps should occur in the series.

- *Step 1, Finding Clue Words*: In Step 1, students learn to find clue words in individual sentences to make guesses about the sentences' hidden meanings. Finding clue words occurs in all of the lessons in the series. You may need two or three Finding Clue Words lessons before you introduce the next step.

- *Step 2, Question Generation*: In Step 2, students learn to ask *wh-* questions (who, what, why, where, when, etc.) about stories, using clue words in the stories, so that their peers can make inferences. You should permit each student to have a turn acting as the teacher for the group by asking questions. Question Generation should occur in four lessons.

- *Step 3, Making Predictions*: In Step 3, you should prepare a story by covering a sentence with white paper or opaque white tape. The students must make predictions about the missing sentence's meaning by looking for clues in surrounding sentences. You should include this activity in one lesson (the last lesson) in the series. Clue Finding and Question Generation naturally lead to this third step when students fill a gap in a story.

A series of lessons would include these three activities, presented at various times across the series. If your students seem to understand well the clue-finding activity in Lessons 1 and 2, you may be able to omit Lesson 3 and move to Question Generation a bit early. So, a series of lessons might look like this:

Lesson 1. Finding Clue Words

Lesson 2. Finding Clue Words

Lesson 3. Finding Clue Words

Lesson 4: Finding Clue Words and Question Generation

Lesson 5: Finding Clue Words and Question Generation

Lesson 6: Finding Clue Words and Question Generation

Lesson 7: Finding Clue Words, Question Generation, and Making Predictions

The result of the series of lessons is that your students become active thinkers about meaning in stories because they have learned about specific actions they can take to construct meaning. First, they learn to look for clues. For example, in the sentence, *Peter the prankster surprised his sister,* you might guide your students to select the words *prankster* and *surprised* as clues to the sentence's meaning (that Peter played a trick on his sister that surprised her). Or, in the sentence *Katie went to get a ladder to rescue her kitten*, the words *ladder* and *rescue* would be useful clues (indicating that the kitten might have climbed somewhere high and then couldn't get back down). See Figure 7–2 for additional examples.

Then, when you move to Question Generation, your clue-seeking students learn to generate questions about the clue words to elaborate on the sentence's meaning. For example, they might ask *What is a prankster?*, *What kind of prank do you think Peter played?*, or *How do you think Peter surprised his sister?* Each of these questions, asked by students of their peers, leads students to link their own prior knowledge to story content and construct gap-filling inferences. Finally, in the last step of the lesson series, you provide students a real gap to fill in a story by covering a sentence. This creates an opportunity for students to use their new clue-finding and question-generating skills to construct meaning. See Figure 7–2 for sentences you can use for Clue Finding and Question Generation.

Cloze-ing Gaps and Checking

Two-Story Clue Hunt and Three-Step Inference Building each requires students to actively look for clues in text, and Three-Step Inference Building also requires students to fill gaps in real text. In this Cloze-ing Gaps activity, these instructional strategies have been combined and used successfully to improve struggling comprehenders' comprehension (Carr, Dewitz, and Patberg 1983). To prepare for this lesson, select a story and cover individual words with opaque tape so that students must look for clues to infer the missing words' meanings. To introduce the activity, tell your students that you are going to give them some stories that are puzzles because they are missing words. Then, explain that your students need to look for clues before and after the blank spaces so that they can make guesses

FIGURE 7–2

Sentences for Clue Finding and Question Generation

Clue words are in italics and inferences are in parentheses.

Peter the *prankster surprised* his *sister*.

(Peter played a trick on his sister, which surprised her!)

Katie went to get a *ladder* to rescue her *kitten*.

(The kitten must have climbed somewhere high, like a tree, for Katie to need a ladder.)

Sarah *forgot* her *umbrella* and got very *wet* today.

(It rained today.)

Forgetful Bobby *borrowed* a *pencil*.

(Bobby forgot his pencil today and needed one to complete a task.)

Sadly, Jamal held his *empty cone* and looked at the *messy sidewalk*.

(Jamal's ice cream fell off of his cone.)

Tommy's *class* saw *chickens* and *cows* on their *trip* today.

(Tommy's class took a field trip to a farm.)

Donna *pedaled* the *fastest* and *won* a prize.

(Donna was in a bicycle race.)

Janet *picked up* the *broken lamp* and put her *ball* away.

(Janet was throwing or kicking her ball in the house and knocked over a lamp, which broke.)

Happily, Steve carried his *package* from the *bookstore*.

(Steve got a new book at the bookstore, which made him happy.)

Mother was *surprised* to see *Rex's paws* on the *counter* next to the *empty cake plate*.

(Rex is an animal, probably a dog, and he ate the cake off of the plate on the counter.)

about what the missing words might be. Once your students make guesses, tell them that they can check their answers by asking themselves these questions (adapted from Carr, Dewitz, and Patberg 1983).

1. Does my answer make sense?

2. Does my answer fit in the sentence?

3. Do I know my answer because of what I already know and because of clues in the story?

4. Is there a clue before the blank space?

5. Is there a clue after the blank space?

6. Did new clues make me change my answer, or did I keep my answer?

After working through the process with your students and scaffolding their understanding, provide them opportunities to practice on their own. This activity can be adapted for multiple instructional formats: you can begin with small-group discussion, you can provide written passages with missing words to individual students and have them write their answers to the questions in journals, you can have students work in pairs, you can work together in whole-group instruction, or you can place puzzle passages with missing words at a literacy center where students can work through the six questions using a rubric at the center.

Closing Notes

Word callers typically need support to turn attention to meaning, especially when meaning is not readily (literally) apparent in text and must be inferred. Further, because they are less likely to juggle multiple, meaning-focused thoughts while reading, these children are less likely to connect text concepts with other ideas in text or with their prior knowledge. The lessons presented in this chapter provide structured, explicit support to shift word callers' attention to meaning through active engagement with text. To develop their inference-making skills, word callers learn to search for text clues, think about their own relevant experiences, and consider how each of these contributes to texts' meanings. Once you have infused the new language into your students' vocabularies—*looking for clue words* or *thinking about their own lives*—you may use these prompts in any instructional context, whether they are in language arts, social studies, math, or science. Inference making supports comprehension across subjects and across the school day, and reminders—whether verbal or visual—will help your students continue to use their new inference-making skills.

The length of each of these instructional interventions varies, from one lesson in Two-Story Clue Hunt to ten lessons in Connecting Lives to Stories. Each of these interventions resulted in improved comprehension and inference making for word callers, using the formats and instructional schedules described here. Select the format that you think best fits your students' needs. If you think your students need a more intensive and scaffolded intervention, try Three-Step Inference Building. If you find that your students have more difficulty with gap-filling inferences, then focus on the interventions that provide more support for this skill, such as Connecting Lives to Stories or Cloze-ing Gaps and Checking. You may have observed that your students seem to need a bit of a nudge to shift their focus from decoding processes to active meaning-construction activities. The Two-Story Clue Hunt and Three-Step Inference Building activities provide explicit meaning-seeking actions to refocus your students' attention to texts' meanings. After you complete these intervention lessons, you can continue to remind students to engage in these activities (finding clue words, generating questions) to ensure that they retain their newfound focus on meaning.

How Does This Help You?

Questions to Consider

- Consider the difference between text-connecting and gap-filling inferences. Have you noticed that your students find one or the other more difficult? Why do you think that is the case?

- What practices have you tried to help students understand how to make inferences? What new insights have you gained from reading this chapter to expand your instruction in inferring?

- At the beginning of the chapter I suggested that reading *is* inferring. Do you agree? Why or why not?

Transactional Strategies Instruction

Because Reading Is a Juggling Act

8

Up to this point we've been talking about individual,
research-tested instructional strategies that you can use to
help shift word callers' focus to meaning. Because poor comprehenders "have a limited, highly passive view of reading as
simple decoding," they "concentrate on decoding words and
often do not make meaning or expect texts to make sense"
(Wilhelm 2001, 33–34). Thus, interventions such as the ones
I shared in earlier chapters are often necessary to help word
callers change directions, that is, to provide an instructional
nudge to shift their focus from decoding to meaning. In earlier
chapters you read about

- an assessment to determine the degree to which word
  callers can consider flexibly the sounds and meanings of
  words, and an intervention to help them do so

- riddle construction and wordplay lessons that help word
  callers think about multiple meanings in text

- scaffolded support for word callers' construction of visual
  and verbal models of texts' meanings

- lessons to foster and support inference making in these
  students.

Each of these interventions targets a particular aspect of word
callers' meaning-processing problems (see Chapters 1 and 2 for
more on word callers' thinking), and all result in improved comprehension. But, there's more to good comprehension than each
of these independent pieces. Our ultimate instructional goal for
word callers is to move them toward active, strategic

processing of text, which does not occur in a piecemeal fashion. Rather, we "want readers to use comprehension strategies flexibly, seamlessly, and independently" (Harvey and Goudvis 2007, 21), "shifting effortlessly from one to another as needed to understand what they read" (Keene and Zimmermann 2007, 28). To illustrate what I (and our esteemed colleagues) mean, consider the following description of skilled reading comprehension.

Expert readers' minds are constantly awash with thoughts, which are the objects of continuous reflection, reaction, and elaboration; that is, skilled comprehenders engage in metacognition—active reflection on their own thinking processes—and they deliberately, and continuously, direct their own cognitive processes toward the goal of meaning making (Pressley and Afflerbach 1995; Pressley and Lundeberg 2008). Skilled comprehenders' minds are *constantly active* while they are reading; they are not just occasionally active when prompted to use a strategy. Instead, skilled comprehenders are continually thinking about text, almost as though they are having a conversation with the text in their heads. They are aware of when, whether, and how they understand a text; they use deliberate strategies to achieve that understanding (without being reminded to do so); and they actively seek to construct meaning as they read.

Reflect for a moment on your own reading. This description captures exactly what you and I, as expert readers, do: we monitor carefully while we read, we react to texts, and we question, reread, summarize, and visualize, making connections between texts and what we already know. I can't tell you how many times I have responded (sometimes verbally!) to texts, made notes in margins, dog-eared the pages, or affixed Post-it notes to my books and articles as I read them. My most-read books and articles have scribbles and tags all over them—evidence of my active processing of the text within them. It is this kind of processing that we need to make evident for our poor comprehenders. We want to help them "peer into the mind of a proficient reader" (Keene and Zimmermann 2007, 10). In this chapter I describe a less well-known, but very effective, method for doing just that: Transactional Strategies Instruction (TSI). And, the good news for us is that TSI is effective in improving word callers' reading comprehension. Before I describe TSI, however, a history minilesson will be helpful to place TSI in the broader context of comprehension strategies instruction.

History Minilesson on Comprehension Instruction

Over the past several years we have heard much about teaching our students to be strategic readers, particularly in response to the surprising, groundbreaking findings of Dolores Durkin (1978–1979), who studied comprehension instruction in elementary classrooms; she found that the predominant instructional move for teachers in her study was asking comprehension questions. That may not seem like a bad idea until you consider that asking comprehension questions is the equivalent of *assessing* comprehension. Teachers were essentially testing comprehension regularly but were doing very little to *teach children how* to comprehend. Fast-forward two decades to 1998. Michael Pressley and his colleagues observed elementary reading instruction to determine what had changed since Durkin's study. Sadly, they observed essentially the same practices: teachers asking students questions about texts with very little instruction about *how* to comprehend them (Pressley et al. 1998). Virtually nothing had changed in twenty years.

I don't know about you, but no amount of quizzing is going to help me learn to engage in a complex task, such as rebuilding a car engine or flying an airplane. (I would argue that reading comprehension is similarly complex in that it requires the integration and coordination of many components for successful performance.) In order to understand the nature of the quiz questions, and do well on the quiz, I would need to have received some instruction first. Comprehension is no different. We cannot expect students to do well on comprehension questions without any instruction in how to comprehend texts.

Fortunately, around the time that Pressley and colleagues replicated Durkin's dismal findings, research on highly skilled comprehenders was yielding important insights about the nature of strategically responsive reading comprehension (e.g., Pearson and Dole 1987; Pearson and Gallagher 1983; Pressley and Afflerbach 1995; see Block and Pressley 2001; Block, Gambrell, and Pressley 2002; and Pressley and Lundeberg 2008, for reviews; also see Pressley, Borkowski, and Schneider 1989, for more about good strategy users). As a result, some terrific professional books emerged that changed the face of comprehension instruction for many teachers: books like *Mosaic of Thought* (Keene and Zimmermann 1997, 2007), *Strategies That Work* (Harvey and Goudvis 2000, 2007), and *Improving Comprehension with Think-Aloud Strategies* (Wilhelm 2001). In these texts we learned about essential components of comprehension instruction, such as

- the importance of fostering metacognition, thinking about one's own thinking, in our students so that they can continually monitor their understanding of text like skilled comprehenders

- teaching the strategies that skilled comprehenders use, such as predicting, making connections, questioning, visualizing, clarifying, and summarizing (see Figure 8–1 on page 113 for brief descriptions of these strategies; Brown 2008; Brown et al. 1996; Duffy 2009; Duke and Pearson 2002; Pressley n.d., 2000; Pressley and Block 2001)

- explicit instruction, otherwise known as thinking aloud, so that skilled readers' invisible mental processes become visible to our students (also see Duffy 2009, for more on explicit instruction)

- gradually releasing responsibility for strategy use so that students have sufficient support for using comprehension strategies before they are expected to apply them independently (see Wilhelm 2001, for a wonderful description of this process).

The research base on comprehension strategies instruction is substantial enough that it was identified by the National Reading Panel (2000) as one of the critical components of literacy instruction for our students. And, the impact of comprehension strategies instruction has been so pervasive that comprehension strategies have even made it into our five most popular core reading programs, albeit in diluted fashion (Dewitz, Jones, and Leahy 2009). Unfortunately, Dewitz and colleagues found that the watered-down versions of strategies instruction in core programs didn't always match well the research-tested strategies instruction in some important ways. This is disheartening: if teachers stick closely to core programs to guide their instruction, we can be virtually guaranteed that their comprehension instruction will not measure up to what the research says works. Thus, the purpose of this chapter is to take a renewed look at the research on effective comprehension instruction and refocus our attention on the active, flexible, integrative nature of skilled comprehenders' strategy use. Integration of strategies in service of comprehension—that's the ultimate goal. Yet, for struggling comprehenders, who demonstrate little awareness of their own thinking, reading is a very passive process (August, Flavell, and Clift 1984; Cain, Oakhill, and Bryant 2004; Garner and Kraus 1981; Paris and Myers 1981). Thus, in order to help these children become successful comprehenders, we must make them aware that reading is *active*, that reading is *thinking*, and that good readers are *always* thinking while reading.

INSIGHTS FROM CHILDREN'S THINKING

In Chapter 2, I described five critical insights from research on children's thinking that enlighten our understanding of struggling comprehenders' difficulties. Each of these can help us understand word callers' difficulties with strategic, meaning-making processes, and TSI can help move word callers in the direction of good comprehenders on each of these dimensions.

- To be strategic readers, children must think about their own thought processes alongside other features like letter-sound information and meaning—that is, they must be able to think about more than one idea at a time—a task that word callers find difficult.

- Word callers' naïve theories about reading get in the way of their understanding of text. Strategic readers define reading as an active process of meaning making, whereas word callers define reading in terms of passive decoding processes.

- Strategic readers are integrative thinkers. They put the pieces of reading tasks together, they integrate meaning components with prior knowledge; and they integrate their strategies in service of good comprehension. Word callers are much more likely to think about single components of reading tasks.

- Strategic readers are deliberate thinkers. They are metacognitively aware of their own mental processes, and they deliberately direct their own thinking toward particular goals. Word callers are much less aware or deliberate in their approach to reading.

- Finally, strategic readers are flexible thinkers. Not only can they coordinate several things in their minds at once, but they can actively switch between those ideas while reading. Word callers, on the other hand, are notoriously inflexible in their approach to reading.

The Research in Favor of TSI

So, what can be done to move children in the direction of active, flexible, strategic comprehension? We must employ classroom practices that help students understand that good readers have a constant running conversation in their minds about texts' meanings. And, teaching one strategy at a time is not always sufficient to help students achieve this awareness. To answer this question Michael Pressley and his colleagues (Brown 2008; Brown et al. 1996; Gaskins et al. 1993; Pressley et al. 1992) developed an instructional procedure that helps students understand and adopt the active, flexible thinking of good comprehenders. To accomplish this, teachers actively engage students in a running conversation about texts' meanings and their own thoughts about those meanings while reading a text. Part of that conversation involves teaching, and coordinating, a small set of strategies known to improve comprehension (see Figure 8–1). This process effectively scaffolds—in actual conversational interactions—the kind of running conversation and active mental processing that occur in skilled comprehenders' minds while reading. Because the instructional procedure involves multiple interactions, or transactions, between the students and text, between students and the teacher, and between students themselves, Pressley and colleagues dubbed it Transactional Strategies Instruction (TSI) to capture the active transactions that

FIGURE 8–1

Descriptions of Research-Tested Comprehension Strategies

1. Predicting: Good readers use clues to make guesses about what will happen in a text, and they update predictions as they read.

2. Making Connections: Good readers think about their own knowledge and experiences and how they relate to information in a text to help them understand text better.

3. Questioning: Good readers ask themselves questions about a text, or wonder about things in a text, and they look for those answers while they read.

4. Visualizing: Good readers create pictures in their minds of what is going on in a text to help them picture what the text means.

5. Summarizing: Good readers remember the most important points in a text that tell what it is about; if they can't remember, they reread so that they can.

6. Clarifying: Good readers notice confusing points in texts and then do things to resolve (or fix) the confusions, such as rereading, looking forward or backward in the text for clues to meaning, or looking at pictures.

are constantly occurring in TSI classrooms. The flavor of this instructional technique may remind you of Reciprocal Teaching, designed by Palincsar and Brown (1984). In fact, Reciprocal Teaching is similar to TSI in that it involves teaching students to coordinate a small set of strategies, rather than focusing on one or two strategies at a time, which is effective in improving poor comprehenders' reading comprehension (Lysynchuk, Pressley, and Vye 1990). However, TSI goes beyond Reciprocal Teaching because it is more adaptive and flexible, and thus more closely approximates the adaptive, flexible, responsive reading behavior of good comprehenders.

Does TSI work? In short, yes. TSI is effective across grade levels and in multiple formats.

- In a yearlong test of TSI with struggling second-grade readers, Brown et al. (1996; also see Brown 2008) found that students taught with TSI were more aware of strategies, were more active strategy users, learned more information from texts, and scored higher on reading comprehension tests, than their peers who received the usual reading instruction.

- Reutzel, Smith, and Fawson (2005) recently compared TSI to single-strategy instruction (in which students were taught one strategy at a time), also with second-grade students. Students in TSI classrooms learned more information in more detail from science texts, and they performed better on measures of comprehension than their peers who experienced single-strategy (instead of integrative) instruction.

- In a recent test of multiple-strategy instruction with third graders, Boulware-Gooden et al. (2007) found that students who were taught to coordinate multiple strategies performed better on tests of vocabulary and reading comprehension than peers who received nonintegrative instruction. (This study was not designed to test TSI per se, but the instructional procedures in the multiple-strategies condition were quite similar to TSI.)

- In a study with slightly older students, Diehl (2005) implemented TSI with fourth- and fifth-grade word callers in a before-school intervention she called the Breakfast Club. Students who participated made gains in motivation and engagement, as well as reading and language arts scores.

- Finally, in studies with struggling adolescent readers, Anderson (1992; Anderson and Roit 1993) found that TSI effectively improved sixth- to eleventh-grade students' comprehension.

Integrating TSI into Your Daily Teaching

As you can see, TSI is effective for students from the primary grades through high school. These findings are quite encouraging, but TSI is not a quick fix. TSI is about changing the *way* you teach, not just changing *what* you teach (as were the lessons presented earlier in this book). Just as students must learn to be active, strategic readers, it takes teachers several semesters—and sometimes years—to become flexible, expert TSI teachers (Brown et al. 1996; Bergman and Schuder 1993; Pressley et al. 1989; Schuder 1993). If you decide to try TSI in your classroom, you might consider working with colleagues to learn to develop these skills. When teachers learning to implement TSI were surveyed about the factors that helped them the most, 97 percent reported that "interaction with other teachers" was most helpful, followed closely by "reading professional articles" at 87 percent (Pressley et al. 1991, 45). Just keep in mind that learning to be an effective TSI teacher is an incremental process, and its effects on your students are worth the effort.

TSI simplifies and focuses comprehension instruction. For example, in many core reading programs, the strategies and skills presented can range in number from fifteen to twenty-nine, which can be unworkable (Dewitz, Jones, and Leahy 2009). TSI focuses on a much smaller set of comprehension strategies known to be supported by research (Brown 2008; Brown et al. 1996; Pressley 2002, 2006b). These are described in Figure 8–1. TSI teachers model the use of these strategies repeatedly (Brown 2008), not occasionally; and "strategies are not taught or practiced in isolation, but rather they are blended into meaning-oriented text discussions" (Brown 2008, 539). Instruction focuses on the orchestration of this small set of strategies (Brown et al. 1996) so that readers' thinking begins to approximate that of skilled comprehenders. To give you an idea of the flavor of TSI in comparison to other instruction, see Figure 8–2 (reprinted from Anderson 1992). The contrasts illustrated in Figure 8–2 demonstrate the goal of TSI: for students to *engage independently in the thinking* that good comprehenders do (not just hear about the thinking or watch you do the thinking). Consider the following examples of comprehension strategies instruction when introducing the book, *Thank You, Mr. Falker*, by Patricia Polacco.

TEACHER A (*Holding up the book*): I wonder what this story is going to be about. Hmmmmm. I'm looking at the cover, and I see a man looking at a girl. The girl looks like she is having a tough time with her schoolwork. Have you ever had a hard time with your schoolwork?

STUDENT: I had a hard time with my math homework yesterday! It took me *forever* to finish.

TEACHER A: Yes, sometimes it takes us a while to learn new things. Good job! Let's look at the title. It says, *Thank You, Mr. Falker.* So that makes me think that maybe this man (*Pointing to the picture on the cover*) is named Mr. Falker, because that's the name in the title. How do you think the girl in the picture is feeling? (*Students respond; teacher repeats their responses.*) Sad. Upset. Unhappy. Good. I think she looks unhappy, too. And, because the title says, "Thank you, Mr. Falker," I'll bet he helps her somehow. What do you think? You think maybe he helps her with her work? (*Students respond.*) Yes. I think so, too. So, I think this book is going to be about a man named Mr. Falker who helps a girl with her schoolwork. That's my prediction. Okay, let's read to see if that prediction is right!

FIGURE 8–2

Teacher Shifts Toward Fostering Active Reading Strategies and Intentional Learning

From	To
1. Focuses on smooth and errorless reading by the students; treats wrong answers as errors to be corrected.	1. Welcomes reading problems and treats them as problem-solving opportunities— as objects of inquiry.
2. Focuses on and provides "right" answers.	2. Focuses on *how to* arrive at answers.
3. Asks content-based and experience-based questions that only apply to the passage at hand.	3. (a) Teaches students to ask questions. (b) Encourages and allows students to model thinking
4. Focuses primarily on students' interests, assuming that learning will take place.	4. Focuses primarily on what students are learning while keeping their interests in mind.
5. Focuses on what students already know.	5. Focuses on new learning.
6. Teaches a strategy in the same way, even after students have mastered it.	6. Upgrades strategy use so that students are continually learning to use a strategy in more complex ways.
7. Models answers.	7. (a) Models thinking. (b) Encourages and allows students to model thinking.
8. Maintains control of what is to be learned.	8. Lets students take control of what is to be learned.
9. Does most of the hard thinking during a reading session.	9. Teaches students to do the hard thinking during a reading session.
10. Emphasizes getting work done and reading finished.	10. Emphasizes learning from what is read and learning about reading.
11. Does not inform students as to the purpose of the reading session.	11. Tells students what they will be learning and why it is worth learning.
12. Focuses primarily on learning the content of what is read.	12. Focuses on reading and learning to read.
13. Avoids teaching during actual reading.	13. Teaches during reading to help clarify difficulties and ensure understanding.
14. Begins reading by asking questions or telling about the text.	14. Begins reading by having students skim to form their own impressions and set their own goals.
15. Begins session with motivators; ends session with questions.	15. Begins session with goal setting and predictions; ends session by returning to goals and predictions.
16. Decides which words and ideas in a text will be difficult, then asks or tells students about them.	16. Teaches students to determine difficult words and ideas.
17. Focuses primarily on individual performance and success.	17. Focuses primarily on group collaboration.
18. Teaches a particular strategy with any passage.	18. Fits the strategy to the passage at hand.
19. Encourages homogeneity in the group so that everyone can show the same accomplishments.	19. Encourages different abilities in the group so that students can share ideas and talents.
20. Presents only easy material.	20. Presents challenging material.

In this instance Teacher A has made a prediction, and she has (minimally) engaged students in *her* discussion about the book. But, she hasn't *explained the reasoning* behind her prediction. Her line of reasoning may seem obvious to you and me, but we are expert comprehenders. This kind of thinking is not often obvious to children who are learning to read, especially children with comprehension problems. Teacher A was modeling the actions and the answer (see number 7, Figure 8–2), but she was not modeling the *thinking* or allowing students to model thinking, either. Now consider Teacher B's classroom.

TEACHER B: Today we are going to read this book (*Holds up* Thank You, Mr. Falker). Remember, good readers are good thinkers. When good readers read, they use strategies to help themselves understand what they are reading. Today we're going to start with the prediction strategy. Do you remember what prediction is? (*Students respond.*) That's right, a prediction is like a guess! When good readers read books, they use clues to make guesses about what a book is about. Making predictions like this helps good readers to understand books better.

Here, the teacher has explicitly told students that readers are thinkers, that strategies help students understand texts, and she has explained what mental processes are involved in prediction—that is, that good readers use clues to make guesses about what books will be about. Finally, the teacher also explained why the prediction strategy is useful: because it can help students understand books better.

TEACHER B (*Continuing*): Let's see, what clues can we use to predict what this book will be about? (*Note that she is having the students do the thinking rather than doing all the thinking herself.*)

STUDENT A: How 'bout the title? That's a good clue. Titles tell what the book is about.

TEACHER B: I like the way you're thinking and looking for clues! We can use the title as a clue, and this title is *Thank You, Mr. Falker.* Tell me what you're thinking about the title.

STUDENT B: Well, when someone says "thank you" it usually means that somebody did something for them or helped them or something. Since the title says "thank you" to a guy named Mr. Falker, I'm thinking that the book is about how Mr. Falker helps somebody.

TEACHER B: So, we can predict that the book might be about a man named Mr. Falker who helps somebody. That's some good predicting, [Student B]! What other clues can we use to make predictions about this book?

STUDENT C: I am looking at the picture. That can be a clue. There's a girl doing work, and she doesn't look very happy!

TEACHER B: Great thinking! The picture can be a clue, too. So, what are you thinking about the girl? Why do you think she doesn't look happy?

STUDENT D: Well, it looks like she doesn't like her work, or maybe she doesn't get it. I was doing a word problem yesterday for math, and I got stuck. I just couldn't figure it out. And, that made me really mad!

TEACHER B: Good thinking, [Student D]! You just used another good reader strategy: making connections. You connected the picture of the girl on the cover to something you experienced yesterday, and that can help you understand the story better. What do you all think about that, about [Student D]'s connection to getting frustrated with his math work?

STUDENT C: Yeah, that's why I think that picture is a good clue, 'cause the girl looks pretty upset. I'm thinking she's having a hard time with her work, and she's mad about it, and maybe that guy Mr. Falker is gonna help her with it. That's what I predict.

TEACHER B: Good thinking, [Student C]. You used the picture clues and [Student D]'s connection to visualize how the girl might be feeling. Visualization is another one of our good reader strategies that helps us understand texts better! So, [Student C] used clues from the picture and title, [Student D]'s connection, and her own visualization to make a prediction about what is going to happen in the book. That's some really good work! Let's read to find out if someone named Mr. Falker helps this girl.

In this classroom, the primary goal is the collaborative construction of meaning, with a clear emphasis on thinking in order to derive meaning from text (not on answering comprehension questions). Teacher B continually refers to students' thinking and opens the conversation to students' reasoning and responses. Engaging in this kind of dialogue about their own thinking about texts' meanings is how students learn to master the running conversations about meaning that occur in the minds of good comprehenders. Students experience this running dialogue in conversation first, with support, and eventually they are able to internalize it (Vygotsky 1962; Wilhelm 2001). Note that Teacher B explicitly explains the reasoning behind the strategy so that students understand *how* to arrive at a prediction, whereas Teacher A just *performed* a prediction without explaining how she got there. Another important point illustrated here is that in TSI classrooms, the teacher is not the sole thinker and modeler. Rather, the students actively participate in thinking, too, which they model for one another as they participate in a dialogue about the text's meaning. For example, at the end of the interaction in Teacher B's classroom, Student C modeled the reasoning processes required to arrive at the prediction, and Teacher B identified those and made sure to explicitly explain them to the class. Finally, note how Teacher B capitalized on teachable moments and highlighted Student D's use of the making-connections strategy, and Student C's use of visualization: instructional moves that will help all the students in the group see how good readers coordinate multiple strategies. However, in Teacher A's classroom when a student connected the girl's expression in the picture to her own experience, Teacher A praised the student's response, but did not identify the connection as a strategic move. And, most important (and detrimental for students), nowhere in Teacher A's comments were there any explicit references to specific aspects of her own, or her students', strategic reasoning.

The Purpose of the Lessons: Helping Word Callers Learn to Use Multiple Comprehension Strategies

TSI engages struggling comprehenders in interactive and integrative strategic discussions that mirror the internal dialogues that occur in skilled readers' minds. By making these dialogues explicit, and teaching children a small array of strategies so that they quickly move to active participation in the dialogues, students receive the scaffolded support necessary to approach text strategically on their own.

The Instructional Strategy: How Might TSI Look in Your Classroom?

The preceding example provides an illustration of what a bit of TSI discussion might sound like in your classroom. Here, I provide a summary description of TSI, outline four critical components of TSI (from Brown 2008), and provide examples so that you can imagine further how this might look in your classroom.

A Summary Description of TSI

The primary goal of TSI is the development of independent readers who understand that *reading is thinking* and that *meaning construction is always central to this process* (Bergman and Schuder 1993; Brown 2008). Word callers clearly need this understanding; thus TSI was designed to help struggling comprehenders experience the kind of active, flexible processing that occurs in skilled comprehenders' minds. This is accomplished by teaching students the six comprehension strategies in Figure 8–1 one at a time and moving to integration and independent use as quickly as possible. TSI lessons engage students in cooperative group dialogues in which group members construct meaning together as they discuss their own strategic responses to text (which is why knowledge of strategies is necessary); and, the discussions themselves are examples of the kind of integrative, internal strategic dialogues that occur in skilled readers' minds. Think of it this way: even with quality instruction of individual strategies, students are not likely to integrate them on their own. We know that gradual release of responsibility is most effective for students (Pearson and Gallagher 1983; Wilhelm 2001), and integration of strategies is no different. Struggling comprehenders need to *see* integration in action and *participate* in the process before they will be able to integrate strategies on their own.

As you might imagine, TSI lessons are necessarily flexible and unstructured, because you cannot create a structured plan for the natural unfolding of a cooperative dialogue. In TSI classrooms you see "a consistent emphasis on the use of cognitive and metacognitive strategies for the construction of understanding" (Gaskins et al. 1993, 301). TSI teachers do not ask questions that have *right* answers (like the traditional comprehension questions Durkin observed in 1978–1979). Rather,

TSI teachers' questions prompt children to think strategically and interact with text as they construct meaning (just as you observed in Teacher B's classroom). Teacher responsiveness is critical to this process. Effective TSI teachers are able to think quickly, explain the reasoning behind their own strategy use, and identify and respond to strategy use in students, while keeping meaning construction central and releasing control for strategy use to students *as quickly as possible*. Rachel Brown (2008) described four dimensions of TSI: the "good strategy user," gradual release of responsibility, collaborative learning, and interpretive discussion. Each of these is described below, and examples of teacher behaviors associated with each dimension are listed in Figure 8–3 (reprinted from Brown 2008).

FIGURE 8–3

Dimensions of Transactional Strategies Instruction

"Good Strategy User" Dimension

- Teachers explain that good readers are strategy users.
- Teachers share their personal experiences with strategy use.
- Teachers point out the importance of thinking while reading.
- Teachers teach students to coordinate their use of several research-based strategies.
- Teachers may emphasize one strategy in a given lesson, but they still model and review other strategies to demonstrate how good readers coordinate their strategy use.
- Teachers emphasize the role of personal choice, effort, and persistence in enacting strategies.
- Teachers motivate students' strategy use by showing how applying strategies improves comprehension.
- Teachers highlight the vital role of prior knowledge activation and connection in comprehension.
- Teachers emphasize how students' knowledge of their strengths and needs as readers can inform the strategic choices they make.
- Teachers stress that good readers set goals for reading, monitor their comprehension, use strategies to overcome difficulties, and evaluate their progress toward goals.

Gradual Release of Responsibility Dimension

- Teachers promote independent strategy use by shifting responsibility for using strategies to students as quickly as possible.
- Teachers explain the benefits of strategy use in general and the value of using specific strategies.

FIGURE 8–3

Gradual Release of Responsibility Dimension, *CONTINUED*

- Teachers describe when (before, during, or after) and where (with fiction or nonfiction texts) to apply strategies.

- Teachers mentally model (e.g., think aloud) to make their thinking apparent to students.

- Teachers explain and model how interpretations are made using comprehension strategies.

- Teachers assist students by (a) cueing them to choose a strategy that makes sense in the context, (b) clarifying through reexplanations, (c) seizing teachable moments, (d) modeling use of strategies repeatedly, and (e) tailoring instruction and tasks to meet students' needs and understanding.

- Teachers provide guided and independent practice so that students learn to use strategies when cued by a diverse array of goals, needs, task demands, and texts.

Collaborative Learning Dimension

- Teachers cue students to support their interpretations by asking "What makes you say so?" or requesting them to use strategies to support their claims, which enables less able students to observe the processes of more capable peers.

- Teachers and students construct meaning together.

- Teachers serve as discussion facilitators, not as directors.

- Teachers avoid scripted lessons. They establish a priori objectives, identify one or two focal strategies for a given lesson, and prearrange where and when to explain and model them. However, the teacher is flexible in meeting set goals, depending on the needs of students and the flow of the interpretive discussion.

Interpretive Discussion Dimension

- Teachers frequently ask "What are you thinking?" and "What are you feeling?"

- Teachers do not direct students toward one "correct" interpretation.

- Teachers promote extended dialogues among participants rather than fostering recitation-style interactions.

- Teachers prepare students for discussion by explaining, modeling, and establishing guidelines for active, equitable, and considerate participation in interpretive discussions.

- Teachers often refrain from adding interpretive responses to minimize the impact of their statements on students' comments.

- Teachers do not say "You're right" or "That's wrong." Instead they restate students' comments to encourage additional responses.

The Four Dimensions of TSI

TSI sounds complex, but don't let that keep you from trying this in your class-room. Typically, in small-group instruction you probably already have discussions with your students, and I am willing to bet that many of those small-group con-versations focus on understanding text. Rather than trying to implement TSI in whole-group format or with all of your smaller, guided-reading groups, you might begin by attempting TSI with just one of your small groups, to see how it works. For the sake of example, let's use the picture book *Wolf!*, by Becky Bloom (1999), which is a delightful story about (you guessed it) a hungry wolf who wanders into a town and goes to a farm where he thinks he will find numerous dinner options. Much to his amazement, the farm animals don't respond to his threats because they are reading! The story goes on to describe how the wolf wants to become a reader, too, so he engages in a series of actions to learn to read and then improve his reading skill: going to school, checking out books at the library, and finally buying his very own book. After much practice, he joins the other farm animals as an "educated animal" and a terrific reader.

Good Strategy Users

TSI teachers help students understand that good readers are good strategy users (Pressley and Afflerbach 1995; Pressley and Lundeberg 2008), and they explain why strategies are useful: because strategies help readers understand the mean-ing of what they read. TSI teachers consistently highlight thinking during lessons, modeling the reasoning behind their own strategy use, and helping students to become aware of, and model, their own thinking—but *meaning is always the primary focus*. Thus, your discussions with students should emphasize that good readers do things in their heads that we can't see, called strategies, which help them understand what they read. And, you should explain the reasoning behind particular strategies, making sure that your students are learning how to use a small set of strategies independently (see Figure 8–1). In a TSI lesson with *Wolf!* you might see this conversation.

TEACHER: Today we're going to read this book (*Holds up book*). Before we start, I'm going to show you something you can do to help you understand the book better. When good readers read, they use their thinking strategies to help them understand. Remember talking about strate-gies? Strategies are things you do in your head to help you understand a book, like predicting. Anybody have a prediction about this book?

STUDENT A: Yeah, I know the title is *Wolf!*, and I see a wolf in the picture, so I can already predict it's about a wolf. But, that picture has a pig on the wolf's head. I, ummm . . .

TEACHER: What do you think about that pig?

STUDENT A: He's like, hugging the wolf's head. And, he's happy. That's not like in *The Three Little Pigs*. Those pigs were scared of the wolf 'cause he was going to eat them!

TEACHER: [Student A] used another good reader strategy. He made a connection to another story he knows: *The Three Little Pigs*. What do you think about that connection?

STUDENT B: I think the wolf in *The Three Little Pigs* was mean. And, like [Student A] said, that pig is hugging the wolf and he's smiling. That clue makes me think this wolf is gonna be a nice wolf instead of mean like that other wolf.

TEACHER: So we have two predictions! That's great thinking: [Student A] noticed that the title and the picture clues make us think this book is going to be about a wolf. And then, [Student A] noticed the pig hugging the wolf, which is another good clue! [Student B]'s connection to *The Three Little Pigs* made him think that maybe this is a friendly wolf. So, that's another prediction. When I saw this book, I noticed that all the animals look happy, too. So that made me predict that the animals might like each other, even the wolf! Let's read and see what we find out. Let us know if we need to update any of our predictions.

Gradual Release of Responsibility

Because the goal of TSI is to develop independent, actively strategic readers, TSI teachers try to move students to independent strategy use as soon as they can. To do this, teachers provide specific strategy knowledge for students (see Figure 8–1); they explain the reasoning behind each strategy as well as the benefits of using each strategy. Consider this conversation as an example.

TEACHER: We've already used two good reader strategies today: predicting and making connections. I'm going to tell you about another strategy that you can use to help you understand this book. This new strategy is called questioning. Good readers will sometimes notice things about stories that make them ask themselves questions. Then they figure out the answers to the questions while they are reading, and it helps them understand the story better. Usually, when I use this strategy, my questions start with "I wonder . . . ," and when I looked at this story, the first question that popped into my mind was, "I wonder why the wolf is holding a book!" So, I noticed something about the book that I wanted to know more about, and then I asked myself a question about it: Why is the wolf holding a book?

STUDENT D: Well I have a connection: I saw some real wolves on TV, on an animal show, and they didn't know how to read. I never saw an animal that could read!

STUDENT E: Yeah, I got that connection, too. I never saw any animals read, so that surprised me to see them looking at that book. So, Ms. Teacher, I have a question, too, why are all those animals reading?

TEACHER: [Student D] and [Student E] used their making-connections strategies to help them figure out what the book is going to be about, which led [Student E] to ask an interesting question: Why are all those animals reading? We will need to read to find out. Does anyone else have a question?

STUDENT D: Yeah, why are some of those animals wearing glasses? I never saw that before either! Let's start reading so we can figure it out!

In this exchange you see the teacher reinforce the importance of strategy use and explicitly note that the students have already used two strategies: predicting and making connections. Then, she introduced a new strategy, questioning, and explained the reasoning behind the strategy. To do the introduction she modeled the questioning strategy explicitly for the students, who began using it independently and integrating it with another strategy: making connections. (See Wilhelm 2001 for more on gradual release of responsibility in think-alouds.)

Collaborative Learning

As these conversational exchanges demonstrate, TSI requires a collaborative approach. Put another way, TSI is not teacher-directed as in Teacher A's classroom, earlier. Although the teacher models and explains when introducing new strategies, he or she quickly releases control to the students so that they directly experience active, strategic processing themselves. As part of this collaborative approach, teachers act as knowledgeable guides, cueing students to use strategies or explain their thinking. They use prompts such as, "What makes you think that?" Consider this exchange that occurred a few pages into *Wolf!*

STUDENT A: Mrs. [Teacher]! (*Interrupting the teacher's oral reading of the story*) We have to update a prediction!

TEACHER (*Cueing the student to support her thinking*): What makes you say that, [Student A]?

STUDENT A: Well, the book just said that the wolf was hungry and he went to the farm to find some food, and then he howled at the animals.

TEACHER (*Reminding the students to go back to the strategy*): The story did say those things. Let's think about this. What prediction should we update?

STUDENT B: Oh, we said he was a nice wolf and we said they all liked each other! So, we need to update that first one because he's not being very nice. He's howling at the other animals, and he wants to eat them.

TEACHER: What do you think, [Student A]?

STUDENT A: Yeah, so we need to maybe predict that the wolf might not be nice. Or maybe he's not nice yet. Maybe he turns nice in the story. Yeah.

TEACHER: So, [Student B] thinks we need to update our prediction that the wolf is nice, and [Student A] suggested that maybe the wolf turns nice in the story. This is good thinking. Good readers update predictions as they read.

STUDENT C: Hey, that makes me have a question. I wonder why the wolf turns nice.

TEACHER: Good job using that new questioning strategy. That's a great question: What kinds of things might make him nice? What kinds of connections can you make here?

STUDENT C: The other animals could share food and then he wouldn't be hungry. I know when people share, that they are nicer to each other.

TEACHER: That's a good connection to what you already knew about sharing. Let's read to see what happens next.

Interpretive Discussion

The last dimension of TSI described by Brown (2008) is interpretive discussion. As you can see from the preceding conversational examples, the group works collectively to interpret text, and strategies are the means to the interpretive end. In other words, *strategy use is not the instructional aim in and of itself.* Rather, teachers equip students with strategies so that they can participate in the active interpretation of text. Instead of offering evaluative feedback (i.e., telling students they are right or wrong), teachers guide students' thinking about the text by prompting strategy use and asking them what the text makes them think, how it makes them feel (Brown 2008). Consider this conversational exchange. The teacher has read much of the story and the wolf has once again arrived at the farm, this time carrying his very own book and after having practiced reading it many times over. The story says that "He lay down on the grass, made himself comfortable, took out his new book, and began to read. He read with confidence and passion, and the pig, the cow, and the duck all listened and said not one word" (Bloom 1999, 19).

STUDENT D: I got an answer to a question!

TEACHER (*Stops reading*): You do? What question?

STUDENT D: We wondered why the wolf turned nice. I bet this is when he turns nice!

TEACHER: What makes you think that?

STUDENT D: He learned how to read, and he's a good reader! I'll bet that made him happy because now the other animals aren't making fun of him!

Across this group lesson, the teacher guides children's thinking, and respects students' contributions. In this example, Student D interrupted the teacher's reading. In many classrooms Student D might have been scolded for the interruption, but in the collaborative TSI framework, the student's contribution is valued and supported.

Closing Notes

TSI is complex, and requires that we release much control to our students, which means that lessons may be unpredictable. We know, however, as skilled comprehenders, that our own responses to texts are often unpredictable and occur as the result of our own integrated, strategic processing. In order to begin to understand the active nature of skilled comprehension, word callers need to *see* the kinds of interactive processes that occur in good comprehenders' minds; and the collaborative discussions in TSI classrooms allow this to happen. With continued introduction and reintroduction of the same, small, coordinated set of strategies, students' own use of the strategies is scaffolded, reinforced, and eventually internalized. As Harvey and Goudvis (2007, 33) noted, "We show kids how strategies overlap and intersect. We demonstrate how readers weave them together for a more engaged, rewarding read." We can't teach children to integrate strategies by teaching the strategies independently. Nor can we teach such integration with explicit modeling alone. Just watching us coordinate strategies doesn't enable our students to do so, and integration surely doesn't emerge without support.

How might TSI work alongside the other interventions presented in this book? Recall that those interventions target particular meaning-focused skills with which word callers have difficulty; thus, they can be used whenever you think your struggling comprehenders might need such targeted assistance. TSI provides the broader instructional context to help support the shift to meaning-focused processing of print. Word callers will need specific interventions like those presented earlier in this book to target particular deficits, but they should also be continually immersed in the interactive, integrative, meaning-focused text discussions necessary to understand strategic processing of text. Weekly opportunities are not enough. (Skilled comprehenders' minds are continually active, not active on a weekly basis.) Thus, these kinds of discussions should occur over days and weeks and months. And, as you improve in your implementation of TSI, and your students can independently use the strategies, such meaning- and thinking-focused text discussion should permeate your instruction and class interaction in multiple contexts: whole-group instruction, small-group instruction, individual interaction, and even across the curriculum (e.g., Reutzel, Smith, and Fawson 2005, showed the superiority of TSI to single-strategy instruction in instruction with science texts). In sum, providing repeated opportunities for word callers to see and hear and participate in the kinds of strategic dialogues that occur continually in the minds of skilled comprehenders will support their own development as strategic meaning makers and improve their comprehension.

How Does This Help You?

Questions to Consider

- How is TSI similar to your current comprehension instruction? How is it different?

- Consider the differences between Teacher A and Teacher B (pp. 115–118). Teacher A "thought aloud" as she *told* her students what *she thought* about the text. In contrast, Teacher B actually *talked about thinking*, with explicit attention to strategies good readers use and the evidence for those in her students' thinking. Reflect on your own comprehension instruction: Is it more similar to that of Teacher A or Teacher B? Why or why not?

- List three ways you could implement some of the objectives of TSI in your own comprehension instruction. You might consider both whole-group and small-group instruction as you make your list.

REFERENCES

Children's Literature Cited

Banks, Kate. 2006. *Max's Words*. New York: Frances Foster Books.

Bell, Cece. 2003. *Sock Monkey Goes to Hollywood*. Cambridge, MA: Candlewick Press.

Bloom, Becky. 1999. *Wolf!* New York: Orchard Books.

Boase, Susan. 2002. *Lucky Boy*. Boston: Houghton Mifflin.

Bridges, Shirin Yim. 2002. *Ruby's Wish*. New York: Scholastic.

Cisco, Cheyenne. 1997. *The Lion and the Mouse*. New York: Sadlier-Oxford.

Kirk, Daniel. 2007. *Library Mouse*. New York: Scholastic.

Lester, Helen. 1988. *Tacky the Penguin*. Boston, MA: Houghton Mifflin.

Parish, Peggy. 1963. *Amelia Bedelia*. New York: HarperCollins.

Polacco, Patricia. 1998. *Thank You, Mr. Falker*. New York: Philomel Books.

Schachner, Judy. 2007. *Skippyjon Jones and the Big Bones*. New York: Scholastic.

Slobodkina, Esphyr. 1968. *Caps for Sale*. New York: HarperCollins.

Steig, William. 1969. *Sylvester and the Magic Pebble*. New York: Aladdin.

Professional Works Cited

Aaron, P. G., R. Malatesha Joshi, and Kathryn A. Williams. 1999. "Not All Reading Disabilities Are Alike." *Journal of Learning Disabilities* 32 (2): 120–37.

Adams, Marilyn J. 1990. *Beginning to Read: Thinking and Learning About Print*. Cambridge, MA: MIT Press.

Afflerbach, Peter, P. David Pearson, and Scott G. Paris. 2008. "Clarifying Differences Between Reading Skills and Reading Strategies." *The Reading Teacher* 61 (5): 364–73.

Allington, Richard L. 1980. "Teacher Interruption Behaviors During Primary Grade Oral Reading." *Journal of Educational Psychology* 72 (3): 371–77.

———. 2006. "Fluency: Still Waiting After All These Years." In *What Research Has to Say About Fluency Instruction*, ed. S. Jay Samuels and Alan E. Farstrup, 94–105. Newark, DE: International Reading Association.

Almasi, Janice F. 2003. *Teaching Strategic Processes in Reading*. New York: Guilford Press.

Anderson, Valerie. 1992. "A Teacher Development Project in Transactional Strategy Instruction for Teachers of Severely Reading-Disabled Adolescents." *Teaching and Teacher Education* 8 (4): 391–403.

Anderson, Valerie, and Marsha Roit. 1993. "Planning and Implementing Collaborative Strategy Instruction for Delayed Readers in Grades 6–10." *The Elementary School Journal* 94 (2): 121–37.

Applegate, Mary D., Anthony J. Applegate, and Virginia Modla. 2009. "'She's My Best Reader; She Just Can't Comprehend': Studying the Relationship Between Fluency and Comprehension." *The Reading Teacher* 62 (6): 512–21.

Arlin, Patricia K. 1981. "Piagetian Tasks as Predictors of Reading and Math Readiness in Grades K–1." *Journal of Educational Psychology* 73 (5): 712–21.

Astington, Janet, Paul L. Harris, and David R. Olson. 1988. *Developing Theories of Mind*. New York: Cambridge University Press.

August, Diane L., John H. Flavell, and Renee Clift. 1984. "Comparison of Comprehension Monitoring of Skilled and Less Skilled Comprehenders." *Reading Research Quarterly* 20 (1): 39–53.

Baker, Linda, and Nancy Stein. 1981. "The Development of Prose Comprehension Skills." In *Children's Prose Comprehension: Research and Practice*, ed. Carol M. Santa and Bernard L. Hayes, 7–43. Newark, DE: International Reading Association.

Baumann, James F., and Bette S. Bergeron. 1993. "Story Map Instruction Using Children's Literature: Effects on First Graders' Comprehension of Central Narrative Elements." *Journal of Reading Behavior* 25 (4): 407–37.

Bayliss, Donna M., Christopher Jarrold, Alan D. Baddeley, and Eleanor Leigh. 2005. "Differential Constraints on the Working Memory and Reading Abilities of Individuals with Learning Difficulties and Typically Developing Children." *Journal of Experimental Child Psychology* 92: 76–99.

Bergman, Janet L., and Ted Schuder. 1993. "Teaching At-Risk Students to Read Strategically." *Educational Leadership* 50 (4): 19–23.

Bialystok, Ellen, and Alison Niccols. 1989. "Children's Control over Attention to Phonological and Semantic Properties of Words." *Journal of Psycholinguistic Research* 18 (4): 369–87.

Biemiller, Andrew. 2001. "Teaching Vocabulary: Early, Direct, and Sequential." *American Educator* 25 (1): 24–28, 47.

———. 2003. "Oral Comprehension Sets the Ceiling on Reading Comprehension." *American Educator* 27 (1): 23, 44.

Bigler, Rebecca S., and Lynn Liben. 1992. "Cognitive Mechanisms in Children's Gender Stereotyping: Theoretical and Educational Implications of a Cognitive-Based Intervention." *Child Development* 63 (6): 1351–63.

Blair, Clancy, and Rachel P. Razza. 2007. "Relating Effortful Control, Executive Function, and False Belief Understanding to Emerging Math and Literacy Ability in Kindergarten." *Child Development* 78 (2): 647–63.

Block, Cathy Collins, and Susan E. Israel. 2004. "The ABCs of Performing Highly Effective Think-Alouds." *The Reading Teacher* 58 (2): 154–67.

Block, Cathy Collins, Sheri R. Parris, and Cinnamon S. Whiteley. 2008. "CPMs: A Kinesthetic Comprehension Strategy." *The Reading Teacher* 61 (6): 460–70.

Block, Cathy Collins, and Michael Pressley. 2001. *Comprehension Instruction: Research-Based Best Practices.* New York: Guilford Press.

Block, Cathy Collins, Linda Gambrell, and Michael Pressley. 2002. *Improving Comprehension Instruction: Rethinking Research, Theory, and Classroom Practice.* San Francisco: Jossey-Bass.

Borduin, Beverly J., Charles M. Borduin, and Christopher M. Manley. 1994. "The Use of Imagery Training to Improve Reading Comprehension of Second Graders." *The Journal of Genetic Psychology* 155 (1): 115–18.

Boulware-Gooden, Regina, Suzanne Carreker, Ann Thornhill, and R. Malatesha Joshi. 2007. "Instruction of Metacognitive Strategies Enhances Reading Comprehension and Vocabulary Achievement of Third-Grade Students." *The Reading Teacher* 61 (1): 70–77.

Briggs, Chari, and David Elkind. 1973. "Cognitive Development in Early Readers." *Developmental Psychology* 9 (2): 279–80.

Brown, Rachel. 2008. "The Road Not Yet Taken: A Transactional Strategies Approach to Comprehension Instruction." *The Reading Teacher* 61 (7): 538–47.

Brown, Rachel, Michael Pressley, Peggy Van Meter, and Ted Schuder. 1996. "A Quasi-Experimental Validation of Transactional Strategies Instruction with Low-Achieving Second-Grade Readers." *Journal of Educational Psychology* 92 (5): 18–37.

Cain, Kate, and Jane Oakhill. 1999. "Inference Making Ability and Its Relation to Comprehension Failure." *Reading and Writing* 11: 489–503.

———. 2003. "Reading Comprehension Difficulties." In *Handbook of Children's Literacy*, ed. Terezinha Nunes, and Peter Bryant. Dordrecht, NL: Kluwer Academic Publishers.

———. 2007. "Reading Comprehension Difficulties: Correlates, Causes, and Consequences." In *Children's Comprehension Problems in Oral and Written Language: A Cognitive Perspective*, ed. Kate Cain and Jane Oakhill, 41–75. New York: Guilford Press.

Cain, Kate, Jane Oakhill, Marcia A. Barnes, and Peter E. Bryant. 2001. "Comprehension Skill, Inference-Making Ability, and Their Relation to Knowledge." *Memory & Cognition* 29 (6): 850–59.

Cain, Kate, Jane Oakhill, and Peter Bryant. 2004. "Children's Reading Comprehension Ability: Concurrent Prediction by Working Memory, Verbal Ability, and Component Skills." *Journal of Educational Psychology* 96: 31–42.

Cain, Kate, Jane Oakhill, and Kate Lemmon. 2004. "Individual Differences in the Inference of Word Meanings from Context: The Influence of Reading Comprehension, Vocabulary Knowledge, and Memory Capacity." *Journal of Educational Psychology* 96 (4): 671–81.

Carlisle, Joanne F. 2000. "Awareness of the Structure and Meaning of Morphologically Complex Words: Impact on Reading." *Reading and Writing: An Interdisciplinary Journal* 12: 169–90.

Carr, Eileen M., Peter Dewitz, and Judythe P. Patberg. 1983. "The Effect of Inference Training on Children's Comprehension of Expository Text." *Journal of Reading Behavior* 15 (3): 1–18.

Cartwright, Kelly B. 1997. "The Role of Multiple Classification Skill in Children's Early Skilled Reading." PhD diss., University of Arkansas.

———. 2002. "Cognitive Development and Reading: The Relation of Reading-Specific Multiple Classification Skill to Reading Comprehension in Elementary School Children." *Journal of Educational Psychology* 94 (1): 56–63.

———. 2006. "Fostering Flexibility and Comprehension in Elementary Students." *The Reading Teacher* 59 (7): 628–34.

———. 2007. "The Contribution of Graphophonological-Semantic Flexibility to Reading Comprehension in College Students: Implications for a Less Simple View of Reading." *Journal of Literacy Research* 39: 173–93.

———, ed. 2008a. *Literacy Processes: Cognitive Flexibility in Learning and Teaching*. New York: Guilford Press.

———. 2008b. "The Role of Cognitive Flexibility in Reading Comprehension: Past, Present, and Future." In *Handbook of Research on Reading Comprehension*, ed. Susan E. Israel and Gerry Duffy, 115–39. Mahwah, NJ: Lawrence Erlbaum Associates.

———. 2008c. "Cognitive Flexibility and Reading Comprehension: Relevance to the Future." In *Comprehension Instruction: Research-Based Best Practices*, 2d ed., ed. C. C. Block and S. R. Parris, 50–64. New York: Guilford Press.

Cartwright, Kelly B., Allison M. Bock, Heather N. Guiffré, and Michael J. Montaño. 2006. "Using Classification Tasks to Assess and Improve Reading-Specific Cognitive Flexibility." *Cognitive Technology* 11 (2): 23–29.

Cartwright, Kelly B., Jan Clause, and Kenneth Schmidt. 2007. "Effects of a Small Group Graphophonological-Semantic Flexibility Intervention on Reading Comprehension in Elementary Students." Paper presented at the National Reading Conference, November 28–December 1, Austin, TX.

Cartwright, Kelly B., and Elizabeth A. Coppage. 2009. "Cognitive Profiles of Word Callers: Cognitive Flexibility, Vocabulary, and Word Identification in Elementary School Aged Good and Poor Comprehenders." Paper presented at the 59th annual meeting of the National Reading Conference/Literacy Research Association, December 2–5, Albuquerque, NM.

Cartwright, Kelly B., Elizabeth A. Coppage, Heather N. Guiffré, and Laura Strube. 2008. "A Comparison of Metacognitive Skills and Cognitive Flexibility in Good and Poor Comprehenders." Paper presented at the 15th annual meeting of the Society for the Scientific Study of Reading, July 10–12, Asheville, NC.

Cartwright, Kelly B., Elizabeth A. Coppage, Laura Strube, and Erin Lewis. 2009. The Development of Graphophonological-Semantic Cognitive Flexibility: Insights from Children's Mistakes. Manuscript in preparation.

Cartwright, Kelly B., Marisa C. Isaac, and Kristina L. Dandy. 2006. "The Development of Reading-Specific Representational Flexibility: A Cross-Sectional

Comparison of Second Graders, Fourth Graders, and College Students." In *Focus on Educational Psychology*, ed. Alea V. Mittel, 173–94. New York: Nova Science.

Cartwright, Kelly B., Timothy R. Marshall, Kristina L. Dandy, and Marisa C. Isaac. 2010. "The Development of Graphophonological-Semantic Cognitive Flexibility and Its Contribution to Reading Comprehension in Beginning Readers." *Journal of Cognition and Development* 11 (1): 61–85.

Catts, Hugh W., Tiffany P. Hogan, and Marc E. Fey. 2003. "Subgrouping Poor Readers on the Basis of Individual Differences in Reading-Related Abilities." *Journal of Learning Disabilities* 36 (2): 151–64.

Center, Yola, Louella Freeman, Gregory Robertson, and Lynne Outhred. 1999. "The Effect of Visual Imagery Training on the Reading and Listening Comprehension of Low Listening Comprehenders in Year 2." *Journal of Research in Reading* 22 (3): 241–56.

Chall, Jeanne S. 1996. *Stages of Reading Development*, 2d ed. Fort Worth: Harcourt Brace.

Chalupa, Nancy. 2008. Email message to author, January 25.

Chinn, Clark A., Martha A. Waggoner, Richard C. Anderson, Marlene Schommer, and Ian A. G. Wilkinson. 1993. "Situated Actions During Reading Lessons: A Microanalysis of Oral Reading Error Episodes." *American Educational Research Journal* 30 (2): 361–92.

Chorzempa, Barbara Fink, and Steve Graham. 2006. "Primary Grade Teachers' Use of Within-Class Ability Grouping in Reading." *Journal of Educational Psychology* 98 (3): 529–41.

Clay, Marie M. 1985. *The Early Detection of Reading Difficulties*, 3d ed. Portsmouth, NH: Heinemann.

———. 1991. *Becoming Literate: The Construction of Inner Control*. Portsmouth, NH: Heinemann.

———. 2001. *Change over Time in Children's Literacy Development*. Portsmouth, NH: Heinemann.

Cohen, S. Alan, Joan S. Hyman, and Edward E. Battistini. 1983. "Effects of Teaching Piagetian Decentration upon Learning to Read." *Reading Improvement* 20 (2): 96–104.

Connor, Carol McDonald, Frederick J. Morrison, Barry J. Fishman, Christopher Schatschneider, and Phyllis Underwood. 2007. "Algorithm-Guided Individualized Reading Instruction." *Science* 315 (26 January): 465–64.

Connor, Carol McDonald, Frederick J. Morrison, and Lisa Slominski. 2006. "Preschool Instruction and Children's Emergent Literacy Growth." *Journal of Educational Psychology* 98 (4): 665–89.

Connor, Carol McDonald, Shayne B. Piasta, Barry Fishman, Stephanie Glasney, Christopher Schatschneider, Elizabeth Crowe, Phyllis Underwood, and Frederick

Morrison. 2009. "Individualizing Student Instruction Precisely: Effects of Child ×
Instruction Interactions on First Graders' Literacy Development." *Child Development* 80 (1): 77–100.

Davidson, Matthew C., Dima Amso, Loren Cruess Anderson, and Adele Diamond.
2006. "Development of Cognitive Control and Executive Functions from 4 to 13
Years: Evidence from Manipulations of Memory, Inhibition, and Task Switching."
Neuropsychologia 44: 2037–2078.

De Beni, Rossana, and Paola Palladino. 2000. "Intrusion Errors in Working
Memory Tasks: Are They Related to Reading Comprehension Ability?" *Learning
and Individual Differences* 12 (2): 131–44.

De Beni, Rossana, Paola Palladino, Francesca Pazzaglia, and Cesare Cornoldi.
1998. "Increases in Intrusion Errors and Working Memory Deficit of Poor Comprehenders." *The Quarterly Journal of Experimental Psychology* 51A (2): 305–20.

De Luca, Cinzia R., Stephen J. Wood, Vicki Anderson, Jo-Anne Buchanan, Tina
M. Proffitt, Kate Mahony, and Christos Pantelis. 2003. "Normative Data from the
Cantab I: Development of Executive Function over the Lifespan." *Journal of Clinical and Experimental Neuropsychology* 25 (2): 242–54.

Dewitz, Peter, and Pamela K. Dewitz. 2003. "They Can Read the Words, but They
Can't Understand." *The Reading Teacher* 56 (5): 422–35.

Dewitz, Peter, Jennifer Jones, and Susan Leahy. 2009. "Comprehension Strategy
Instruction in Core Reading Programs." *Reading Research Quarterly* 44 (2): 102–26.

Diehl, Holly L. 2005. "Snapshots of Our Journey to Thoughtful Literacy." *The Reading Teacher* 59 (1): 56–69.

diSessa, Andrea A. 2006. "A History of Conceptual Change Research: Threads and
Fault Lines." In *The Cambridge Handbook of the Learning Sciences*, ed. R. Keith
Sawyer, 265–81. New York: Cambridge University Press.

diSessa. Andrea A., Nicole M. Gillespie, and Jennifer B. Esterly. 2004. "Coherence
Versus Fragmentation in the Development of the Concept of Force." *Cognitive Science* 28 (6): 843–900.

Dolch, Edward. 1960. *Teaching Primary Reading*, 3d ed. Champaign, IL: Garrard
Press.

Doughty, David. 2009. Personal communication to author, April 25.

Duffy, Gerald. 2009. *Explaining Reading: A Resource for Teaching Concepts, Skills,
and Strategies*, 2d ed. New York: Guilford Press.

Duffy, Gerald G., Laura R. Roehler, and Beth Ann Herrmann. 1988. "Modeling
Mental Processes Helps Poor Readers Become Strategic Readers." *The Reading
Teacher* 41 (8): 762–67.

Duffy, Gerald G., Laura R. Roehler, Eva Sivan, Gary Rackliffe, Cassandra Book,
Michael S. Meloth, Linda G. Vavrus, Roy Wesselman, Joyce Putnam, and Dina
Bassiri. 1987. "Effects of Explaining the Reasoning Associated with Using Reading
Strategies." *Reading Research Quarterly* 22 (3): 347–68.

Duke, Nell K., and P. David Pearson. 2002. "Effective Practices for Developing Reading Comprehension." In *What Research Has to Say About Reading Instruction*, ed. Alan E. Farstrup and S. Jay Samuels, 205–42. Newark, DE: International Reading Association.

Durik, Amanda M., Mina Vida, and Jacquelynne S. Eccles. 2006. "Task Values and Ability Beliefs as Predictors of High School Literacy Choices: A Developmental Analysis." *Journal of Educational Psychology* 98 (2): 382–93.

Durkin, Dolores. 1978–1979. "What Classroom Observations Reveal About Reading Comprehension Instruction." *Reading Research Quarterly* 14 (4): 481–533.

Ehrlich, Marie-France, Martine Remond, and Hubert Tardieu. 1999. "Processing of Anaphoric Devices in Young Skilled and Less Skilled Comprehenders: Differences in Metacognitive Monitoring." *Reading and Writing: An Interdisciplinary Journal* 11: 29–63.

Flavell, John H.1988. "The Development of Children's Knowledge About the Mind: From Cognitive Connections to Mental Representations." In *Developing Theories of Mind*, ed. Janet W. Astington, Paul L. Harris, and David R. Olson, 244–67. New York: Cambridge University Press.

———. 2004. "Theory-of-Mind Development: Retrospect and Prospect." *Merrill-Palmer Quarterly* 50 (3): 274–90.

Flavell, John H., Patricia H. Miller, and Scott A. Miller. 2002. *Cognitive Development*, 4th ed. Upper Saddle River, NJ: Prentice Hall.

Flood, James, Diane Lapp, Sharon Flood, and Greta Nagel. 1992. "Am I Allowed to Group? Using Flexible Patterns for Effective Instruction." *The Reading Teacher* 45 (8): 608–16.

Fry, Edward, and Jacqueline Kress. 2006. *The Reading Teacher's Book of Lists.* San Francisco: Jossey-Bass.

Garner, Ruth, and Catherine Kraus. 1981. "Good and Poor Comprehender Differences in Knowing and Regulating Reading Behaviors." *Educational Research Quarterly* 6 (4): 5–12.

Garon, Nancy, Susan E. Bryson, and Isabel M. Smith. 2008. "Executive Function in Preschoolers: A Review Using an Integrated Framework." *Psychological Bulletin* 134 (1): 31–60.

Gaskins, Irene W., Richard C. Anderson, Michael Pressley, Elizabeth A. Cunicelli, and Eric Satlow. 1993. "Six Teachers' Dialogue During Cognitive Process Instruction." *The Elementary School Journal* 93 (3): 277–304.

Gaskins, Robert, and Irene W. Gaskins. 1997. "Creating Readers Who Read for Meaning and Love to Read: The Benchmark School Reading Program." In *Instructional Models in Reading*, ed. Steven A. Stahl and David. A. Hayes, 131–59. Mahwah, NJ: Lawrence Erlbaum Associates.

Gernsbacher, Morton Ann, and Rachel R. W. Robertson. 1995. "Reading Skill and Suppression Revisited." *Psychological Science* 6 (3): 165–69.

Gersten, Russell, Lynn S. Fuchs, Joanna P. Williams, and Scott Baker. 2001. "Teaching Reading Comprehension Strategies to Students with Learning Disabilities: A Review of Research." *Review of Educational Research* 71 (2): 279–320.

Golbeck, Susan L. 1983. "Reconstructing a Large-Scale Spatial Arrangement: Effects of Environmental Organization and Operativity." *Developmental Psychology* 19 (4): 644–53.

Gopnik, Alison M., Andrew N. Meltzoff, and Patricia K. Kuhl. 1999. *The Scientist in the Crib: Minds, Brains, and How Children Learn*. New York: William Morrow.

Graesser, Arthur C., Murray Singer, and Tom Trabasso. 1994. "Constructing Inferences During Text Comprehension." *Psychological Review* 101 (3): 371–95.

Guajardo, Nicole R., Jessica Parker, and Kandi Turley-Ames. 2009. "Associations Among False Belief Understanding, Counterfactual Reasoning, and Executive Function." *British Journal of Developmental Psychology* 27 (3): 681–702.

Hansen, Jane. 1981. "The Effects of Inference Training and Practice on Young Children's Reading Comprehension." *Reading Research Quarterly* 16 (3): 391–417.

Hansen, Jane, and P. David Pearson. 1983. "An Instructional Study: Improving the Inferential Comprehension of Good and Poor Fourth-Grade Readers." *Journal of Educational Psychology* 76 (6): 821–29.

Harris, Karen R., and Michael Pressley. 1991. "The Nature of Cognitive Strategy Instruction: Interactive Strategy Construction." *Exceptional Children* 57 (5): 392–404.

Hart, Betty, and Todd R. Risley. 1995. *Meaningful Differences in the Everyday Experiences of Young American Children*. Baltimore: Brookes Publishing.

Harvey, Stephanie, and Anne Goudvis. 2000. *Strategies That Work*. Portland, ME: Stenhouse.

———. 2007. *Strategies That Work*, 2d ed. Portland, ME: Stenhouse.

Hirsch, E. D. Jr. 2003. "Reading Comprehension Requires Knowledge—of Words and the World: Scientific Insights into the Fourth-Grade Slump and the Nation's Stagnant Comprehension Scores." *American Educator* (Spring): 10.

Hughes, Claire. 2002. "Executive Functions and Development: Why the Interest?" *Infant and Child Development* 11: 69–71.

Idol-Maestas, Lorna. 1985. "Getting Ready to Read: Guided Probing for Poor Comprehenders." *Learning Disability Quarterly* 8 (4): 243–54.

Idol, Lorna. 1987. "Group Story Mapping: A Strategy for Both Skilled and Unskilled Readers." *Journal of Learning Disabilities* 20 (4): 196–205.

Idol, Lorna, and Valerie J. Croll. 1987. "Story-Mapping Training as a Means of Improving Reading Comprehension." *Learning Disability Quarterly* 10 (3): 214–29.

Inhelder, Barbel, and Jean Piaget. 1964. *The Early Growth of Logic in the Child*, trans. E. A. Lunzer and D. Papert. New York: Humanities Press.

Israel, Susan E., Cathy Collins Block, Kathryn Bauserman, and Kathryn Kinnucan-Welsch. 2005. *Metacognition in Literacy Learning: Theory, Assessment, Instruction, and Professional Development*. Mahwah, NJ: Lawrence Erlbaum Associates.

Jacques, Sophie, and Philip D. Zelazo. 2005. "On the Possible Roots of Cognitive Flexibility." In *The Development of Social Cognition and Communication*, ed. Bruce D. Homer and Catherine S. Tamis-LeMonda, 53–81. Mahwah, NJ: Lawrence Erlbaum Associates.

Jenkins, Joseph R., James D. Heliotis, Marcy L. Stein, and Mariana C. Haynes. 1987. "Improving Reading Comprehension by Using Paragraph Restatements." *Exceptional Children* 54 (1): 54–59.

Juel, Connie, and Cecilia Minden-Cupp. 2000. "Learning to Read Words: Linguistic Units and Instructional Strategies." *Reading Research Quarterly* 35 (4): 458–92.

Kaiser, Mary Kister, Dennis R. Proffitt, and Michael McCloskey. 1985. "The Development of Beliefs About Falling Objects." *Perception and Psychophysics* 38 (6): 533–39.

Kane, Michael J., Bradley J. Poole, Stephen W. Tuholski, and Randall W. Engle. 2006. "Working Memory Capacity and the Top-Down Control of Visual Search: Exploring the Boundaries of 'Executive Attention.'" *Journal of Experimental Psychology: Learning, Memory and Cognition* 32 (4): 749–77.

Katz, Lauren A., and Joanne F. Carlisle. 2009. "Teaching Students with Reading Difficulties to Be Close Readers: A Feasibility Study." *Language, Speech, and Hearing Services in Schools* 40: 325–40.

Keenan, Thomas, Ted Ruffman, and David R. Olson. 1994. "When Do Children Begin to Understand Logical Inference as a Source of Knowledge?" *Cognitive Development* 9 (3): 331–53.

Keene, Ellin Oliver, and Susan Zimmermann. 1997. *Mosaic of Thought: Teaching Comprehension in a Reader's Workshop*. Portsmouth, NH: Heinemann.

———. 2007. *Mosaic of Thought: The Power of Comprehension Strategy Instruction*, 2d ed. Portsmouth, NH: Heinemann.

Kintsch, Walter. 1994. "Text Comprehension, Memory, and Learning." *American Psychologist* 49 (4): 294–303.

Kloo, Daniela, and Josef Perner. 2003. "Training Transfer Between Card Sorting and False Belief Understanding: Helping Children Apply Conflicting Descriptions." *Child Development* 74 (6): 1823–1839.

Kuhn, Deanna, and Maria Pease. 2006. "Do Children and Adults Learn Differently?" *Journal of Cognition and Development* 7 (3): 279–93.

Kuhn, Melanie R., and Steven A. Stahl. 2003. "Fluency: A Review of Developmental and Remedial Practices." *Journal of Educational Psychology* 95 (1): 3–21.

LaBerge, David, and S. Jay Samuels. 1974. "Toward a Theory of Automatic Information Processing in Reading." *Cognitive Psychology* 6 (2): 293–323.

Laing, Sandra P., and Alan G. Kamhi. 2002. "The Use of Think-Aloud Protocols to Compare Inferencing Abilities in Average and Below-Average Readers." *Journal of Learning Disabilities* 35 (5): 436–47.

Leach, Jennifer M., Hollis S. Scarborough, and Leslie Rescorla. 2003. "Late-Emerging Reading Disabilities." *Journal of Educational Psychology* 95 (2): 211–24.

Lesaux, Nonie, Orly Lipka, and Linda S. Siegel. 2006. "Investigating Cognitive and Linguistic Abilities That Influence the Reading Comprehension Skills of Children from Diverse Linguistic Backgrounds." *Reading and Writing* 19: 99–131.

Levin, Joel R. 1973. "Inducing Comprehension in Poor Readers: A Test of a Recent Model." *Journal of Educational Psychology* 65 (1): 19–24.

Levorato, M. Chiara, Maja Roch, and Barbara Nesi. 2007. "A Longitudinal Study of Idiom and Text Comprehension." *Journal of Child Language* 34: 473–94.

Lynch, Leslie. 2009. Personal communication to author, February 21.

Lysynchuk, Linda M., Michael Pressley, and Nancy J. Vye. 1990. "Reciprocal Teaching Improves Standardized Reading-Comprehension Performance in Poor Comprehenders." *The Elementary School Journal* 90 (5): 469–84.

Martin, Nicole M., and Nell K. Duke. In press. "Interventions to Enhance Informational Text Comprehension." In *Handbook of Reading Disabilities Research*, ed. Richard Allington and Anne McGill-Franzen. London: Routledge.

McCoach, D. Betsy, Ann A. O'Connell, and Heather Levitt. 2006. "Ability Grouping Across Kindergarten Using an Early Childhood Longitudinal Study." *The Journal of Educational Research* 99 (6): 339–46.

McCutchen, Deborah, Becky Logan, and Ulrike Biangardi-Orpe. 2009. "Making Meaning: Children's Sensitivity to Morphological Information During Word Reading." *Reading Research Quarterly* 44 (4): 360–76.

McGee, Anna, and Heather Johnson. 2003. "The Effect of Inference Training on Skilled and Less Skilled Comprehenders." *Educational Psychology* 23 (1): 49–59.

Megherbi, Hakima, and Marie-France Ehrlich. 2005. "Language Impairment in Less Skilled Comprehenders: The On-line Processing of Anaphoric Pronouns in a Listening Situation." *Reading and Writing* 18: 715–53.

Mertzman, Tania. 2008. "Individualising Scaffolding: Teachers' Literacy Interruptions of Ethnic Minority Students and Students from Low Socioeconomic Backgrounds." *Journal of Research in Reading* 31 (2): 183–202.

Mesmer, Heidi Anne E., Katie Dredger, and Mary Alice Barksdale. 2008. "Guys Read: Overcoming the Opportunity Gap." Paper presented at the 58th annual meeting of the National Reading Conference, December 3–6, Orlando, FL.

Nagy, William. 2007. "Metalinguistic Awareness and the Vocabulary-Comprehension Connection." In *Vocabulary Acquisition: Implications for Reading Comprehension*, ed. Richard K. Wagner, Andrea E. Muse, and Kendra R. Tannenbaum, 52–77. New York: Guilford Press.

Nagy, William, Virginia W. Berninger, and Robert D. Abbott. 2006. "Contributions of Morphology Beyond Phonology to Literacy Outcomes of Upper Elementary and Middle School Students." *Journal of Educational Psychology* 98 (1): 134–47.

Nation, Kate. 2005. "Children's Reading Comprehension Difficulties." In *The Science of Reading: A Handbook*, ed. Margaret J. Snowling and Charles Hulme, 248–65. Hoboken, NJ: Wiley-Blackwell.

Nation, Kate, and Margaret J. Snowling. 1998. "Individual Differences in Contextual Facilitation: Evidence from Dyslexia and Poor Reading Comprehension." *Child Development* 69 (4): 996–1011.

———. 1999. "Developmental Differences in Sensitivity to Semantic Relations Among Good and Poor Comprehenders: Evidence from Semantic Priming." *Cognition* 70: B1–B13.

———. 2000. "Factors Influencing Syntactic Awareness Skills in Normal Readers and Poor Comprehenders." *Applied Psycholinguistics* 21: 229–41.

Nation, Kate, Paula Clarke, and Margaret J. Snowling. 2002. "General Cognitive Ability in Children with Reading Comprehension Difficulties." *British Journal of Educational Psychology* 72: 549–60.

National Reading Panel. 2000. *Report of the National Reading Panel: Teaching Children to Read: An Evidence-Based Assessment of the Scientific Research Literature on Reading and Its Implications for Reading Instruction: Reports of the Subgroups.* Washington, DC: National Institute of Child Health and Human Development, National Institutes of Health.

Oakhill, Jane. 1982. "Constructive Processes in Skilled and Less Skilled Comprehenders' Memory for Sentences." *British Journal of Psychology* 73: 13–20.

———. 1983. "Instantiation in Skilled and Less-Skilled Comprehenders." *Quarterly Journal of Experimental Psychology* 35A: 441–50.

———. 1984. "Inferential and Memory Skills in Children's Comprehension of Stories." *British Journal of Educational Psychology* 54: 31–39.

———. 1993. "Children's Difficulties in Reading Comprehension." *Educational Psychology Review* 5 (3): 223–37.

Oakhill, Jane, and Sima Patel. 1991. "Can Imagery Training Help Children Who Have Comprehension Problems?" *Journal of Research in Reading* 14: 106–15.

Oakhill, Jane, and Nicola Yuill. 1986. "Pronoun Resolution in Skilled and Less-Skilled Comprehenders: Effects of Memory Load and Inferential Complexity." *Language and Speech* 29 (1): 25–37.

———. 1996. "Higher Order Factors in Comprehension Disability: Processes and Remediation." In *Reading Comprehension Difficulties: Processes and Intervention*, ed. Cesare Cornoldi and Jane Oakhill, 69–92. Mahwah, NJ: Lawrence Erlbaum Associates.

Oakhill, Jane, Joanne Hartt, and Deborah Samols. 2005. "Levels of Comprehension Monitoring and Working Memory in Good and Poor Comprehenders." *Reading and Writing* 18: 657–86.

Oakhill, Jane, Nicola Yuill, and Alan Parkin. 1986. "On the Nature of the Difference Between Skilled and Less-Skilled Comprehenders." *Journal of Research in Reading* 9 (2): 80–91.

Palincsar, Annemarie, and Ann L. Brown. 1984. "Reciprocal Teaching of Comprehension-Fostering and Comprehension-Monitoring Activities." *Cognition and Instruction* 1 (2): 117–75.

Paris, Scott G., and Janis E. Jacobs. 1984. "The Benefits of Informed Instruction for Children's Reading Awareness and Comprehension Skills." *Child Development* 55 (6): 2083–2093.

Paris, Scott G., and Meyer Myers II. 1981. "Comprehension Monitoring, Memory, and Study Strategies of Good and Poor Readers." *Journal of Reading Behavior* 13 (1): 5–22.

Pearson, P. David, and Janice Dole. 1987. "Explicit Comprehension Instruction: A Review of Research and a New Conceptualization of Instruction." *The Elementary School Journal* 88 (2): 151–65.

Pearson, P. David, and Margaret C. Gallagher. 1983. "The Instruction of Reading Comprehension." *Contemporary Educational Psychology* 8: 317–44.

Piaget, Jean, and Barbel Inhelder. 1969. *The Psychology of the Child*, trans. Helen Weaver. New York: Basic Books (original work published 1966).

Pilonieta, Paola, and Adriana L. Medina. 2009. "Reciprocal Teaching for the Primary Grades: 'We Can Do It, Too!'" *The Reading Teacher* 63 (2): 120–29.

Pressley, Michael. *Comprehension Strategies Instruction*. www.msularc.org/docu/5-page_comprehension.pdf (accessed June 5, 2009).

———. 1976. "Mental Imagery Helps Eight-Year-Olds Remember What They Read." *Journal of Educational Psychology* 68 (3): 355–59.

———. 2000. "What Should Comprehension Instruction Be the Instruction Of?" In *Handbook of Reading Research, Volume III*, ed. Michael Kamil, Peter B. Mosenthal, P. David Pearson, and Rebecca Barr, 545–61. Mahwah, NJ: Lawrence Erlbaum Associates.

———. 2002. "Comprehension Strategies Instruction: A Turn of the Century Status Report." In *Comprehension Instruction: Research-Based Best Practices*, ed. Cathy Collins Block and Michael Pressley, 11–27. New York: Guilford Press.

———. 2006a. *Reading Instruction That Works: The Case for Balanced Teaching*, 3d ed. New York: Guilford Press.

———. 2006b. "What the Future of Reading Research Could Be." Paper presented at the International Reading Association Reading Research conference, April 29, Chicago.

Pressley, Michael, and Peter Afflerbach. 1995. *Verbal Protocols of Reading: The Nature of Constructively Responsive Reading*. Hillsdale, NJ: Lawrence Erlbaum Associates.

Pressley, Michael, and Cathy Collins Block. 2001. "Summing Up: What Comprehension Could Be." In *Comprehension Instruction: Research-Based Best Practices*, ed. Cathy Collins Block and Michael Pressley, 383–92. New York: Guilford Press.

Pressley, Michael, John G. Borkowski, and Wolfgang Schneider. 1989. "Good Information Processing: What It Is and How Education Can Promote It." *International Journal of Educational Research* 13: 857–67.

Pressley, Michael, Nell K. Duke, Irene W. Gaskins, Lauren Fingeret, Juliet L. Halladay, Yonghan Park, Lindsey Mohan, Katherine R. Hilden, Shenglan Zhang, Kelly Reffitt, Lisa M. Raphael, Julia Reynolds, Deborah Golos, Kathryn L. Solic, and Stephanie Collins. 2008. "Working with Struggling Readers: Why We Must Get Beyond the Simple View of Reading and Visions of How It Might Be Done." In *Handbook of School Psychology*, 4th ed, ed. Terry B. Gutkin and Cecil R. Reynolds, 522–46. New York: Wiley.

Pressley, Michael, Pamela Beard El-Dinary, Irene Gaskins, Ted Schuder, Janet L. Bergman, Janice Almasi, and Rachel Brown. 1992. "Beyond Direct Explanation: Transactional Instruction of Reading Comprehension Strategies." *The Elementary School Journal* 92 (5): 513–55.

Pressley, Michael, Irene W. Gaskins, Elizabeth A. Cunicelli, Nancy J. Burdick, Margaret Schaub-Matt, Deborah S. Lee, and Nancy Powell. 1991. "Strategy Instruction at Benchmark School: A Faculty Interview Study." *Learning Disability Quarterly* 14 (Winter): 19–48.

Pressley, Michael, Fiona Goodchild, Joan Fleet, Richard Zajchowski, and Ellis D. Evans. 1989. "The Challenges of Classroom Strategy Instruction." *The Elementary School Journal* 89 (3): 301–42.

Pressley, Michael, Katherine Hilden, and Rebecca Shankland. 2005. *An Evaluation of End-Grade-3 Dynamic Indicators of Basic Early Literacy Skills (DIBELS): Speed Reading Without Comprehension, Predicting Little.* East Lansing: Michigan State University Literacy Achievement Research Center. www.msularc.org/docu/dibels_submitted.pdf (accessed July 24, 2009).

Pressley, Michael, and Mary Lundeberg. 2008. "An Invitation to Study Professionals Reading Professional-Level Texts: A Window on Exceptionally Complex, Flexible Reading." In *Literacy Processes: Cognitive Flexibility in Learning and Teaching*, ed. Kelly B. Cartwright, 165–87. New York: Guilford Press.

Pressley, Michael, Ruth Wharton-McDonald, Jennifer Mistretta-Hampston, and Marissa Echevarria. 1998. "Literacy Instruction in 10 Fourth- and Fifth-Grade Classrooms in Upstate New York." *Scientific Studies of Reading* 2 (2): 159–94.

Reiter, Astrid, Oliver Tucha, and Klaus W. Lange. 2004. "Executive Functions in Children with Dyslexia." *Dyslexia* 11: 116–31.

Reutzel, D. Ray, John A. Smith, and Parker C. Fawson. 2005. "An Evaluation of Two Approaches for Teaching Reading Comprehension Strategies in the Primary Years Using Science Information Texts." *Early Childhood Research Quarterly* 20: 276–305.

Ricketts, Jessie, Kate Nation, and Dorothy V. M. Bishop. 2007. "Vocabulary Is Important for Some, but Not All Reading Skills." *Scientific Studies of Reading* 11 (3): 235–57.

Riddle Buly, Marsha, and Sheila Valencia. 2002. "Below the Bar: Profiles of Students Who Fail State Reading Assessments." *Educational Evaluation and Policy Analysis* 24 (3): 219–39.

Rubman, Claire N., and Harriet Salatas Waters. 2000. "A, B Seeing: The Role of Constructive Processes in Children's Comprehension Monitoring." *Journal of Educational Psychology* 92 (3): 503–14.

Sadoski, Mark. 1983. "An Exploratory Study of the Relationships Between Reported Imagery and the Comprehension and Recall of a Story." *Reading Research Quarterly* 19 (1): 110–23.

———. 1985. "The Natural Use of Imagery in Story Comprehension and Recall: A Replication and Extension." *Reading Research Quarterly* 20 (5): 658–67.

Samuels, S. Jay. 2002. "Reading Fluency: Its Development and Assessment." In *What Research Has to Say About Reading Instruction*, ed. Alan E. Farstrup and S. Jay Samuels, 166–83. Newark, DE: International Reading Association.

Sawyer, R. Keith, ed. 2006. *The Cambridge Handbook of the Learning Sciences*. New York: Cambridge University Press.

Schuder, Ted. 1993. "The Genesis of Transactional Strategies Instruction." *The Elementary School Journal* 94 (2): 183–200.

Shankweiler, Donald, Eric Lundquist, Leonard Katz, Karla K. Stuebing, Jack M. Fletcher, Susan Brady, Anne Fowler, Lois G. Dreyer, Karen E. Marchione, Sally E. Shaywitz, and Bennett E. Shaywitz. 1999. "Comprehension and Decoding: Patterns of Association in Children with Reading Difficulties." *Scientific Studies of Reading* 3 (1): 69–94.

Siegler, Robert S. 2000. "The Rebirth of Children's Learning." *Child Development* 71 (1): 26–35.

Springer, Ken, and Frank C. Keil. 1989. "On the Development of Biologically Specific Beliefs: The Case of Inheritance." *Child Development* 60: 637–48.

St. Clair-Thompson, Helen L., and Susan E. Gathercole. 2006. "Executive Functions and Achievements in School: Shifting, Updating, Inhibition, and Working Memory." *The Quarterly Journal of Experimental Psychology* 59 (4): 745–59.

Sternberg, Robert J., and G. Reid Lyon. 2002. "Making a Difference in Education: Will Psychology Pass Up the Chance?" *Monitor on Psychology* 33 (7): 76.

Stothard, Susan E., and Charles Hulme. 1992. "Reading Comprehension Difficulties in Children: The Role of Language Comprehension and Working Memory Skills." *Reading and Writing: An Interdisciplinary Journal* 4: 245–56.

Swanson, H. Lee, Crystal B. Howard, and Leilani Sáez. 2007. "Reading Comprehension and Working Memory in Children with Learning Disabilities in Reading." In *Children's Comprehension Problems in Oral and Written Language: A Cognitive Perspective*, ed. Kate Cain and Jane Oakhill, 157–85. New York: Guilford Press.

Talbott, Elizabeth, John Wills Lloyd, and Melody Tankersley. 1994. "Effects of Reading Comprehension Interventions for Students with Learning Disabilities." *Learning Disability Quarterly* 17 (3): 223–32.

Teale, William H., and Elizabeth Sulzby, eds. 1986. *Emergent Literacy: Writing and Reading*. Norwood, NJ: Ablex.

Tomesen, Marieke, and Cor Aarnoutse. 1998. "Effects of an Instructional Programme for Deriving Word Meanings." *Educational Studies* 24 (1): 107–28.

Tomlinson, Carol Ann. 1999. *The Differentiated Classroom: Responding to the Needs of All Learners*. Alexandria, VA: Association for Supervision and Curriculum Development.

Torppa, Minna, Asko Tolvanen, Anna-Maija Poikkeus, Kenneth Eklund, Marja-Kristiina Lerkkanen, Esko Leskinen, and Heikki Lyytinen. 2007. "Reading Development Subtypes and Their Early Characteristics." *Annals of Dyslexia* 57: 3–32.

Trench, Nicki. 2005. *The Cool Girl's Guide to Knitting: Everything the Novice Knitter Needs to Know*. Bath, UK: Parragon.

Unsworth, Nash, and Randall W. Engle. 2008. "Speed and Accuracy of Accessing Information in Working Memory: An Individual Differences Investigation of Focus Switching." *Journal of Experimental Psychology: Learning, Memory, and Cognition* 34 (3): 616–30.

van der Schoot, Menno, Alain L. Vasbinder, Tako M. Horsley, Albert Reijntjes, and Ernest C. D. M. van Lieshout. 2009. "Lexical Ambiguity Resolution in Good and Poor Comprehenders: An Eye Fixation and Self-Paced Reading Study in Primary School Children." *Journal of Educational Psychology* 101 (1): 21–36.

Vygotsky, Lev S. 1962. *Thought and Language*. Cambridge, MA: MIT Press.

Wanzek, Jeanne, and Sharon Vaughn. 2007. "Research-Based Implications from Extensive Early Reading Interventions." *School Psychology Review* 36 (4): 541–61.

Wellman, Henry M., and Susan A. Gelman. 1992. "Cognitive Development: Foundational Theories of Core Domains." *Annual Review of Psychology* 43: 337–75.

Wellman, Henry M., and David Liu. 2004. "Scaling of Theory-of-Mind Tasks." *Child Development* 75 (2): 523–41.

Whitehurst, Grover J., and Christopher J. Lonigan. 1998. "Child Development and Emergent Literacy." *Child Development* 69 (3): 848–72.

Wilhelm, Jeffrey D. 2001. *Improving Comprehension with Think-Aloud Strategies: Modeling What Good Readers Do*. New York: Scholastic.

———. 2002. *Action Strategies for Deepening Comprehension: Role Plays, Text Structure Tableaux, Talking Statues, and Other Enrichment Techniques That Engage Students with Text*. New York: Scholastic.

Woodcock, Richard W. 1987. *Woodcock Reading Mastery Tests—Revised*. Circle Pines, MN: American Guidance Service.

Yuill, Nicola. 1996. "A Funny Thing Happened on the Way to the Classroom: Jokes, Riddles, and Metalinguistic Awareness in Understanding and Improving Poor Comprehension in Children." In *Reading Comprehension Difficulties: Processes and Intervention*, ed. Cesare Cornoldi and Jane Oakhill, 193–220. Mahwah, NJ: Lawrence Erlbaum Associates.

———. 2007. "Visiting Joke City: How Can Talking About Jokes Foster Metalinguistic Awareness in Poor Comprehenders?" In *Reading Comprehension Strategies: Theories, Interventions and Technologies*, ed. Danielle S. McNamara. Mahwah, NJ: Lawrence Erlbaum Associates.

Yuill, Nicola, and Trish Joscelyne. 1988. "Effect of Organizational Cues and Strategies on Good and Poor Comprehenders' Story Understanding." *Journal of Educational Psychology* 80 (2): 152–58.

Yuill, Nicola, Lucinda Kerawalla, Darren Pearce, Rose Luckin, and Amanda Harris. 2008. "Using Technology to Teach Flexibility Through Peer Discussion." In *Literacy Processes: Cognitive Flexibility in Learning and Teaching*, ed. Kelly B. Cartwright, 320–41. New York: Guilford Press.

Yuill, Nicola, and Jane Oakhill. 1988. "Effects of Inference Awareness Training on Poor Reading Comprehension." *Applied Cognitive Psychology* 2: 33–45.

———. 1991. *Children's Problems in Text Comprehension: An Experimental Investigation*. Cambridge: Cambridge University Press.

Yuill, Nicola, Jane Oakhill, and Alan Parkin. 1989. "Working Memory, Comprehension Ability and the Resolution of Text Anomaly." *British Journal of Psychology* 80: 351–61.

Zabrucky, Karen. 1990. "Evaluation of Understanding in College Students: Effects of Text Structure and Reading Proficiency." *Reading Research and Instruction* 29 (4): 46–54.

Zabrucky, Karen, and DeWayne Moore. 1989. "Children's Ability to Use Three Standards to Evaluate Their Comprehension of Text." *Reading Research Quarterly* 24 (3): 336–52.

Zelazo, Philip D., Ulrich Müller, Douglas Frye, and Stuart Marcovitch. 2003. "The Development of Executive Function in Early Childhood." *Monographs of the Society for Research in Child Development* 68 (3, Serial No. 274).

Zipke, Marcy. 2007. "The Role of Metalinguistic Awareness in the Reading Comprehension of Sixth and Seventh Graders." *Reading Psychology* 28: 375–96.

———. 2008. "Teaching Metalinguistic Awareness and Reading Comprehension with Riddles." *The Reading Teacher* 62 (2): 128–37.

Zipke, Marcy, Linnea C. Ehri, and Helen Smith Cairns. 2009. "Using Semantic Ambiguity Instruction to Improve Third Graders' Metalinguistic Awareness and Reading Comprehension: An Experimental Study." *Reading Research Quarterly* 44 (3): 300–21.

DAY-BY-DAY SMALL-GROUP READING INTERVENTIONS

Powerful Intervention Strategies for Your Classroom

- Daily, small-group interventions help struggling readers read on level by spring.
- The use of trade books and leveled books reinforces and extends guided reading instruction.
- Practical classroom-tested teaching tools include 100+ pages of reproducibles for teachers and students.

PLUS! Live-from-the-classroom video clips show the lessons in action.

Empowering Professional Development for Your School

- A clear consistent framework fosters schoolwide coherence and continuity.
- A month-by-month planning guide helps organize teaching across grade levels.
- Video clips of the lessons encourage group analysis.
- Dynamic Internet and consulting services support professional learning communities.

"When we're true to children's developmental levels, know which books to put in their hands and provide effective instruction, a lot of good things fall into place. The key is to focus on the children and the practices we know help them to read at each grade level."

—Barbara M. Taylor

To learn more about the series' research base and related efficacy studies visit heinemann.com

Heinemann
DEDICATED TO TEACHERS